First Edition, 2014

Layout: Matthew J. Lucio
Cover: Genesis Design
        www.genesisdesign.com

Font: Hoefler Text.

ISBN: 978-0-9841386-7-8
Published by Balm and Blade Publishing
1927 Mountain Road
Hamburg, PA 19526
www.balmandblade.com

END

Matthew J. Lucio

BALM AND BLADE
PUBLISHING

I am grateful...

    ...to Laura for wearing the name so well
    ...to Aerith, my flower girl
    ...to Artemis, great among the Ephesians.

How to Use This Book
(Step One: This Side Up)

Let's be honest: There are enough books on how to interpret Revelation. I don't mean that all of the answers are out there, but some are certainly better than others. If the goal is to provide resources to people in order to help them understand these twenty-two chapters, then we've succeeded — and failed.

Failed, because which of the 5,000-plus results for "revelation commentary" on amazon.com will you start with in your bid to learn what that one verse means? While only a fraction of those results are even remotely useful, having too many resources can be just as bad as having too few. How can you sort through it all? It overwhelms and intimidates the spiritually curious.

I'm sure every author quite humbly believes their work is indispensable to the study of Revelation, but I'll just point you to some that I've found valuable:

1. *Revelation: Four Views*, Steve Gregg
2. *Revelation of Jesus Christ*, Ranko Stefanovic
3. *Triumph of the Lamb*, Dennis E. Johnson

If you're serious about it, those are great places to start. I don't agree with any of the authors all of the time, but part of being an adult — yeah, even a mature Christian — is learning to accept the good and reject the bad. (That little life lesson is also helpful to apply to the eating of pineapple.) So go read in that direction if you just want A = B.

My little book is to kindle the fire of your desire for truth. I want you to go on to understand Revelation because you love it. This book is the introduction.

"Revelation, meet the reader."
"Reader, meet Revelation."

There we go. These words simply reflect my emotional and literary experience in reading Revelation. My hope is that you can glean some ideas for your own studies and jumpstart your imagination.

I also hope that my experience with Revelation will inspire your own adventures. Play with Revelation. Immerse yourself in it. Enjoy the drama. Love the uncertainty. Be humble and open and ask lots and lots of questions. Go ahead and ask a few more questions. Annoy your friends. Troll your pastor by demanding to know everything about the three unclean spirits which are somehow kind of froggy. "Frogs, pastor, frogs!!!!! What are we going to do?????"

Now get on with it. No grand promises here. No over-selling. Flip through this book, then buy it if you like it. Stop trying to figure out what school of thought I belong to. Any scholar worth her salt should probably encourage you to use this book for actual kindling. Don't worry about following your favorite, brand-name expositors and just relax. Pretend you're new here, because you are.

Enter the world of Revelation for yourself. Allow yourself to be mystified and emboldened and broken, in doubt and in love.

Only then can you really understand any of this stuff. Only then is it worth understanding.

Pro

There are some neighborhoods you just run through. They're unsafe and lifeless. They make the city look bad. You don't have to live in the area very long before word starts getting out about where those neighborhoods are. You figure it out when you ask a stranger for directions and he pauses as if to give you a chance to change your mind about going there. Or it's the subtle way your friend insists that the other store is 'nicer.' It's the reason you get on the highway and get off one exit out of your way. Every big town has those places, but after a while we can forget they're even there. We routine our lives around them. We hardly even notice them anymore.

Revelation is one of those neighborhoods most of us have routined our lives around.

Of course, there are plenty of places in Bible City that seem "run down" besides Revelation. It's usually a chapter or a story that seems out of sync with the overall message of the Bible — like seeing a mud hut next to a Gothic cathedral. I am talking about the texts that tell women not to braid their hair or forbid people from wearing clothes blended from two materials. That's not to say there aren't decent explanations for those things, but the fact that you have to stop and dissect them makes it like driving through mud. We assume that the Bible should be a simple literary pleasure and that there shouldn't be texts that — at least superficially — muddy the waters with big footnotes and debatable opinions. It makes for a poor story. We would hate to read a novel where we had to brake every few chapters and read another book or essay just to make sense of the original paragraph. It's the literary version of riding with someone who is learning to drive a stick shift, hopping down the road like Bugs Bunny, while we carrot curse under our breath...and pray. Plus, there are some texts we would be offended if asked to memorize, and we glide over them when we're reading, to say nothing about reading them out loud in church. But Revelation is a whole book of stuff we generally avoid if we can. The suburb of Psalms is so much nicer.

> *"And the smoke of their torment will rise for ever and ever.*
> *There will be no rest day or night."*
> - Rev. 14.11

It doesn't help that some of the people who love Revelation are strange. You've seen the sort: they wear sandwich boards proclaiming the end is near or sport crazy hair and talk glowingly of Armageddon. They crank on: "I'd hate to be a part of [insert political party/lifestyle/gender/religion here] when the end comes!" Others fill the gaps between asking for money with dire pronouncements of judgment. Revelation becomes a political statement which should dictate American foreign policy. And then you have the people who became convinced that after 2,000 years they alone have discovered the truth and you're not a true Christian until you accept it, too.

Yep...a lot of interesting people live in the neighborhood.

And the popular media coverage doesn't help either, mind you.

That's not to say there aren't some kind, honest souls who have an address there. And it doesn't mean that there aren't a lot of easy-to-grasp, even beautiful parts of Revelation. It's just that reading Revelation forces us to confront the reality that we really don't understand the Bible. Not entirely. Not as much as we pretend. We have the verses we like, the really clear ones, and some trivia we like to rehearse for people in order to burnish our saintly credentials. We know a lot about a little of the Bible. We're happy with Noah's Ark, the Prodigal Son, and that Golden Rule thing. These are the quaint, bite-sized vistas that we put on the Christian postcards ("Come visit Bible City!). But there's more to the Bible. There's more to this city of strange inspiration.

There's Revelation...

And in the very beginning of this neighborhood stands a sign which destroys so many of our assumptions about the place:

> *"The Revelation from Jesus Christ, which God gave him to show*
> *his servants what must soon take place." –* Rev. 1.1

Revelation is meant to reveal something about Jesus we need to know.
Revelation is meant to be understood by all of Jesus' followers.
Revelation is relevant. Whatever is going on in there is happening soon.

So why doesn't Jesus just come out and say it? I mean, for being a book that professes to reveal the truth, it sure seems to go to great length to conceal it behind impossible images of monsters and locusts and mythical cities and seals and horses. It can be frustrating!

Yet as much as we might want to ignore Revelation or yell into the wind for it to yield up its secrets, it is futile. Revelation will not be bought or threatened. It is stubbornly virtuous and enchanting and aflame. It promises to tell us the future. It promises to show us something about Jesus that we didn't get in the previous 65 books. It's tempting to finish Jude and shrug, "I think I know Jesus well enough without Revelation."

But Revelation will not allow you to ignore it. It promises to complete the map showing us the way home, because the way home goes through Revelation's neighborhood. The way forward to Jesus, the way that has been winding from the first fragile pages of peace in Genesis, down through the valleys of kings and conquerors, up the slopes of Galilee in the Gospels, through the Roman roads — the arteries of empire — by which men conquered and were in turn conquered by the first missionaries, runs on through the haunted woods of Revelation. Will you really follow Jesus through all of that and stop now?

Whether we like it or not; whether we're ready for it or not, the road to understanding the Bible and Jesus and the universe leads us through this book. And the road isn't safe. We might find something there that turns everything upside down. We might find our own weaknesses in light of the Lion who hunts in the tall grass. We might see a side of God that's wild and frightening. We might feel our pride flailed by our ignorance. We might not come out of this the same as we entered. But stick to the path. Be brave! For

the best is yet to come.

I
Embers

I, John, your brother and companion in the suffering and kingdom and patient endurance that are ours in Jesus, was on the island of Patmos because of the word of God.

- Revelation 1.9

On one hand, being exiled to a Greek island can't be a bad thing, am I right? I can think of a lot worse places to be forced to live, like under a bridge in Cincinnati or anywhere else in Cincinatti. So when the disciple John tells us that he has been exiled to the island of Patmos because of his faith, you might be tempted to think of it as a forced retirement. After all, the man has to be in his eighties or so. Maybe it's time to relax and turn the keys over to the next generation of up-and-coming leaders. You've worked hard, John. It's time to retire with grace and start writing books on leadership theory and generational change.

But exile is no picnic. Legend has it that the Roman Emperor Domitian first tried to kill John by dropping him in a cauldron of boiling oil. (Olive oil is great for your skin, right?) John survived. What do you do with people you cannot kill? Exile. Ship them away to some ocean-besieged rock where they can't stir up any trouble. Keep them from everyone they love. Prevent them from being in a position of influence. Patmos is the stony spine of a drowned giant in some Greek fantasy. It's barren and boring. Here it was that John seemed condemned to live out his remaining years, isolated and alone and unable to guide the fledgling group of believers with first-hand memories of Jesus any longer.

That's hard.

It was 60 years after John's dearest friend had left him and the other disciples and headed back to heaven. Along the way, all of John's fellow followers had died. Some had their heads chopped off. Some were crucified like their master. Some were stoned to death or impaled with a spear. Not many died of old age, and now John alone remained. It's not easy for the founders of any organization to let go of the reins and let the next generation take control of your baby. These were converted Greeks and Latins who were leading the church—men and women who never met Jesus and who were about as Jewish as baklava. They were disconnected from his heritage; men and women John would find it hard to relate to. All John could do is watch from his place of exile. Patmos.

It was there that Jesus found him and gave him this Revelation and instructed him to "write on a scroll what you see and send it to the seven churches: to Ephesus, Smyrna, Pergamum, Thyatira, Sardis, Philadelphia, and Laodicea" (1.11). Revelation is a letter first and foremost to these seven churches. The road that connected these churches in ancient Asia Minor (modern Turkey) formed a circuit through which the letter would travel. It hasn't stopped circulating.

Question: Which of you, wanting to send a letter, would entrust it to a man very much not in favor with the empire which tried to kill him and then stranded him on an island?

Answer: No one.

It would be like telling a detainee in Guantanamo Bay to write something down and mail it to various U.S. cities. Maybe it'd work, but not without a bunch of eyes, uh, eyeing your letter while thinking very hard about passing it on or not. There are easier ways to get a message out.

Seriously, couldn't Jesus have given this message to someone who wasn't in the imperial *domus canina*? Undoubtedly, there were more efficient ways of getting a letter written and passed around, but Jesus loved John. He wanted to show him he wasn't suffering alone, that he hadn't abandoned him and that his greatest role was still to come.

Revelation is about comebacks; it's about Jesus finding us in our place of exile to show us that he hasn't forgotten us. John's ministry wasn't over. He wasn't "your grandfather's pastor." John, the old dude on Patmos, was given the most contemporary message for the third and fourth generation Christians. The book is also about Jesus' comeback. "If I go," Jesus had told his disciples, "I will come back and take you to be with me that you also may be where I am." Revelation is about Jesus' comeback.

Revelation is also about stirring the embers and getting the fire started again. It shows us that no one, no matter how marginalized they are, is useless to Jesus. He can find us and make use of us wherever we are—even stranded on an island, sidelined by the greatest superpower in the world. God can use that person. We are not in danger of being useless, except by our own unwillingness. Even exile can be opportunity.

Even if the world forgets you, God doesn't. Let him stir the embers of your heart — then watch your world catch fire.

2
Audio

Blessed is the one who reads aloud the words of this prophecy, and blessed are those who hear it and take to heart what is written in it, because the time is short.

- Revelation 1.3

There are some books that don't seem like they were meant to be read, like this set of Edward Gibbons' *Decline and Fall of the Roman Empire* sitting on my shelf. It's covered in this pool-table quality felt and sweetly gilded with gold accents. They are the nicest-looking books I own. But when I started reading it I realized it all rubbed off too easily. I guess they were only meant to stand tall on my shelf and tell people how I had such great taste and broad interests. Bookshelf candy.

Revelation is not one of those books. Revelation is meant to be read out loud.

John tells us that there is this mysterious enchantment that surrounds the book:

> *"Blessed is the one who reads aloud the words of this prophecy, and*
> *Blessed are those who hear it and take to heart what is written in it,*
> *because the time is short."*

But that can't be right, can it? The word "blessed" means "favored" or "fortunate." The words people usually use to describe Revelation are kin to these:

Strange. Scary. Confusing.

Jonathan Kirsch sums up the feeling of many:

> *Revelation, quite in contrast to the Gospels, is notoriously lacking in loving-kindness. Rather, it is a punishing text, full of rage and resentment, almost toxic in its longing for bloody revenge against one's enemies.*

There's something wrong here. Revelation is meant to be a blessing. Next to Jesus' "blessed are the poor in spirit" and "blessed are the pure in heart" is Revelation's "blessed are those who read this book." But few read it. Fewer still walk away feeling particularly blessed.

There's a certain degree of faux spirituality that results in Christians believing they know Jesus and the Bible but becoming less and less interested in reading it. We know Jonah and the fish. We know the story of Esther. We know Elijah on Mount Carmel. And yet when we pick up the Bible, we tend to retrace our steps, preferring to dig in the same fields for the same food. We need spiritual curiosity. We need to be brave. We need Leviticus, Micah, Ezekiel, Daniel, and those books whose names we struggle to locate, if not pronounce. We need them because God is in those books. They offer us a picture of our God we don't get anywhere else.

We need to read Revelation because there is a spiritual treasure in store for those who are brave enough. We can't give up. Is your bag of joy so full it cannot contain any more? Is your spiritual table so burdened with blessings that you have lost your appetite? Do you know Jesus so well that you are satisfied with your relationship? Don't you thirst for something more? Aren't you lacking something? It's like finishing *The Fellowship of the Ring* and walking away from the series. "I know these characters as well as I care. I hope they make it to Mordor and it all works out for them." Don't you want to see how it all turns out?

Endeavor to adventure in this book. Jesus will reveal himself to you in subtle and profound ways. And you will be blessed.

This is the first of seven blessings in the Book of Revelation.

Revelation was meant to be read out loud

    with a voice bold and unafraid.

3
Clark Kent

Coming out of his mouth was a sharp, double-edged sword. His face was like the sun shining in all its brilliance.

- Revelation 1.16

This isn't Jesus. Not the one we remember. This isn't the Jesus we usually see, gently healing someone or cradling a wayward lamb or looking compassionately on the suffering. There's nothing wrong with those things, of course, but they don't show the whole picture. Revelation balances it out.

The first time we see Jesus in Revelation, we see something very different:
- Eyes like fire
- Snow white hair
- Face like the sun
- Holding stars in his hand
- Feet like bronze glowing white-hot in the furnace
- Voice like a waterfall
- A sharp sword came out of his mouth

This Jesus is intimidating. This is the risen Christ whom Mary did not recognize. This isn't the one that's safe. This is Aslan, the untamed lion, who can come and go as he pleases, without owing an explanation to anyone. The Jesus of the Gospels we have willfully misunderstood. We've witnessed his sufferings and mistook them for misfortune. But he was ever in control, choosing the pain, going where he knew he was not welcomed. Though it seems like Jesus is constantly on the run from the religious leaders (and even his own supporters), we must recognize that Jesus was the one leading. No one ever forced Jesus to do something that was outside of his plan.

Everyone thought they could manipulate Jesus. Judas set out to betray him, but ended up betraying his own soul. The Sadducees became trapped in their own web. The Pharisees and Romans finally managed to kill Jesus, but that turned out to be the worst mistake of all because the resurrected Christ reclaimed his unbridled divinity. Jesus' enemies worked tirelessly and cleverly to place Jesus exactly where he wanted to be. Jesus was never closer to his mission than when his enemies sought to derail it.

And now we see Jesus as he is, as he is meant to be seen. His ascension wasn't an escape; it was taking the strategic high ground. Jesus has always been in control of the world and we missed it. We've misunderstood humility for weakness and thought people who loved could be so easily predicted and used. We were wrong. That's not how the universe works.

This vision of Jesus demonstrates that.

Even John falls at his feet, still and terrified. This is the same John referred to in the Gospel as "the disciple whom Jesus kept on loving." John knew Jesus, and yet this vision of Jesus terrified him. It was as if he were a stranger. This wasn't a back-slapping reunion. This was love in its grand divinity.

We all need this. We all need our fading portraits of Jesus to be painted over with a fresh revelation. We need to be constantly reminded that Jesus doesn't exist in simply human clothes, words, or customs. He is more than human. He is Power beyond power; Love beyond love.

Before Jesus gets into the beasts and all of the cryptic stuff, he wants John (and us) to see him for who he really is and understand:

I am God and I'm on your side. No matter what you've suffered and no matter what the future holds, don't forget that all of my power is poured out for you. Let them come. Let them try. They will only drive you closer to Me.

4
Church Fail

I know your deeds, that you are neither cold nor hot. I wish you were either one or the other! So, because you are lukewarm—neither hot nor cold—I am about to spit you out of my mouth. You say, 'I am rich; I have acquired wealth and do not need a thing.' But you do not realize that you are wretched, pitiful, poor, blind and naked...

- Revelation 3.15-17

These churches have problems. That much is clear. Shouldn't it concern us that so many people are wishing to go back to the early church as a model? On one hand, the early church was a place of power — a power our churches seem to lack today. People were healed and did extraordinary things. Purity brings power, right?

Except the early church was seriously messed up. Paul — who visited more of these churches than anyone — was beside himself when he wrote to the Corinthian church that *"it is actually reported that there is sexual immorality among you, and of a kind that even pagans do not tolerate: A man is sleeping with his father's wife. And you are proud! Shouldn't you rather have gone into mourning and have put out of your fellowship the man who has been doing this?"* Incest? And I thought my church had problems...

Then we come to Revelation, where the church in Ephesus is criticized for having "left their first love" while Pergamum got it for "holding to the teaching of Balaam, who taught Balak to entice the Israelites to sin so that they ate food sacrificed to idols and committed sexual immorality." Wait, what? What kind of members are in that church??????

It doesn't get any better in Thyatira, when Jesus describes his problem with them: "I have this against you: you tolerate that woman Jezebel, who calls herself a prophet. By her teaching she misleads my servants into sexual immorality." Ok, I'm noticing a theme...

No place tops the last church, however. The Laodicean Christians were so self-deceived that it's the only church Jesus had nothing nice to say about. He threatened "to spit you out of my mouth" and called them "wretched, pitiful, poor, blind, and naked."

Fathom this: this church was so spiritually bankrupt that they somehow managed to look at their bank accounts and mistake their poverty as riches. Like Don Quixote, they were tilting at windmills.

Look, here's the point: no time period — not even the rainbow-gilded 1950s — hosted the perfect church. While the early church did amazing things as a result of their faithfulness to Jesus, there was also an astonishing level of unfaithfulness. Do you really want to go back there?

The Church must be refounded in every age. We need new men and women to rise up and lay the foundation anew with fresh faithfulness. The proper (and only) valid response to the church's present brokenness is sorrow, not the escapism of pining for the past. So many have been hurt and scarred by Christians in every generation that it demands we own up to our failings in the present by seeking to be presently faithful. They made mistakes back then, too. So let's focus on going forward.

It is also no use merely pointing out the problems in your church. Jesus is better at pointing out problems than you are, and yet he still loves the church. His approach to church is to work patiently and tirelessly for reform. Is there a limit to Jesus' patience? Certainly. But it must be our policy to never give up on God's people before he does. We must have his patience and passion for repentance. We must not have a cold, callous desire for reform. Hear Jesus when he says "those whom I love I rebuke and discipline" (3.19). We want to see people change because we love people and because it breaks our heart to see them act in ways that separate themselves from Jesus. Work toward building the church that God is building. We can't give up on the people he is interceding for. Heaven knows that you and I may need such mercy some day — we've needed it in the past.

The church has problems because the church has people. We have to come to grips with the fact that the church is always broken and always perfect. It is thing between between heaven and earth — with its feet on the earth and its head in the clouds.

5
Church Win

To the one who is victorious, I will give the right to sit with me on my throne, just as I was victorious and sat down with my Father on his throne.

- Revelation 3.21

It is only in coming from the grim reality of the church defeated that we can appreciate the promises Jesus declares at the end of each of these church messages. They are like Christmas presents awaiting us beneath dead trees. Their beauty causes them to stand out, begging us to unwrap and receive them.

Jesus here acts like a parent trying to encourage his child to eat their broccoli and offering a million dollars if they do it. Of course, as a parent you could make them. You could argue that it's good for them, and they will thank you later. You could say that they should eat their broccoli, considering all you've done for them. How reckless is Jesus then, that he should be so extravagant in rewarding us to do what's in our best interest, anyway? Jesus ends every message to his churches with a shameless promise like these:

> To Ephesus...to those who are victorious, I will give the right to eat from the tree of life.

> To Smyrna...the one who is victorious will not be hurt at all by the second death.

> To Thyatira...to the one who is victorious and does my will to the end, I will give authority over the nations.

> To Laodicea...to the one who is victorious I will give the right to sit with me on my throne, just as I was victorious and sat down with my Father on his throne.

Sin is always self-destructive. It diminishes our flourishing as human beings like the cold closes the peeking flower. It wrecks relationships and lowers quality of life. Jesus pleads with us to abandon our course of self-annihilation in exchange for lavish banquets of life. Shouldn't I give up sin because it's bad for me? What further reward do I need? And yet Jesus promises that if I accept his help in overcoming sin that I can sit on the throne with him?

No! I don't deserve it! Let it be enough for me that I accept his grace. I need no further honor. He is doing me an immeasurable service by lending his strength to me that I may overcome my addiction to my own death. And yet Jesus cannot help but to stretch such a fantastic vision of heaven across our skies so golden that it both fills and empties us. We read these promises and our hearts leap, "I want that life! I want to overcome! I want to soar and thrive! I want more than this"

You see, if we're stuck looking at all of the problems, we can become overly critical. We can become talented in finding flaws, when God has always meant for us to be experts in grace. Jesus never finds flaws except to offer his help. After pointing at me, he always points back at himself. We should be the same way, resisting the temptation to merely draw battle lines and play "heroes and villains" in the church. Jesus' blistering broadside against sin in the church was followed by the medicine of his overwhelming grace. The needle must be followed by the cure. This is the model we must follow: for all we discipline or rebuke, we must work twice as hard to extend mercy and love to them. Let us never criticize someone for the wrong they do unless we also are praying for them, lest we grow to take a silent delight in their wrongness.

May God grant us the grace today to be graceful to others. May he grant us the courage to encourage people to be better; to convict and then comfort; to break in order to bind.

Revelation is a book given to help people become victorious!

6
Throne

There before me was a throne in heaven with someone sitting on it.

- Revelation 4.2

After some recreational Googling (a future Olympic sport), I came across this paint-by-numbers version of Da Vinci's Mona Lisa. For those who have actual artistic talent and thus don't know, painting by numbers is a scheme to help the unskilled feel, well, a little less unskilled (I should add that it's meant mainly for children). Numbers on a drawing indicate which color goes where and the finished product looks vaguely like the original masterpiece. But this Mona Lisa was of a higher class. Sure, only twelve colors are apparently needed to repaint the most famous painting in the world, but it had this brilliant gold frame which was just glam enough to convince your gullible friend that you had stolen the original from the Louvre.

At the heart of Revelation, however, is a picture that defies a paint-by-numbers scheme. For that matter, it frustrates our attempts to paint-by-language, too. John struggles to translate for us what he sees, using the word "like" seven times in the first seven verses of chapter four.

A voice like a trumpet.
A rainbow like an emerald.
A surface like a sea of glass.

These similes are the marks of John clawing at the truth, trying as best as he can to find the shape, color, and sound in human experience that can carry the meaning. He doesn't see a creature that was a lion, only one that looks like a lion. We don't know how closely it resembled a lion or in what way. Perhaps it was the tail that convinced John, or the approximate size. What we do know is this:

> *There was a beauty here beyond us. It is beyond brush strokes and our pallid palettes. It cannot be copied, framed, or shared. It is art outside our experience.*

It is the presence of God.

Deep in the center of John's vision is the very throne. It is the center of gravity in the scene. But the one sitting upon the throne isn't named. He has "the appearance of jasper and ruby" — more grasping for words. John doesn't even stretch his imagination in saying "one sat there." No names. To ask who it was upon the throne (if you must) is the wrong question. This vision is about the fact that it's not about Him. He's not the focus here. He's a number that doesn't get painted.

John goes on, speaking of a rainbow as bright as an emerald over the throne. It was a promise of life. Rainbows — that ancient symbol of a promise God once made to an old sailor — come and go, from the skies and our memories. This promise. He rules and is known by his promises. Even if we forget, he doesn't.

The paint is still flowing: in front of this throne are seven lamps blazing, reflecting off of the floor, a peaceful sea of glass. Around the throne are four living creatures, strange and exotic and yet somehow familiar. These are the "Praetorians" of the palace, tasked with guarding their king and reveling in his glory. Unable to contain their joy, they burst out in praise so effusive and genuine that the other beings of the cosmos cannot help but join in. With them are the 24 elders, dressed in robes, as white as light, and crowned — these are the first wave of those humans who will overcome Satan and triumph, to be placed forever near the throne they desperately struggled against sin for.

John's words fill our imagination with fire and glass, strange creatures, ethereal choruses, lightning and worship. But he struggles to relay all of this to us. He's constantly comparing what he sees to what we know, but he is clearly overwhelmed. We can feel his inadequacy, perhaps even his frustration, as he wrestles with the fact that

> heaven is too wonderful for us to understand.

John reaches deep into his bag-o-words to find the richest approximations, but utterly fails to transfer what he saw to our imaginations. It's not that he didn't use the right words, it's that there are no right words. Divine glory sheds our words like an umbrella sheds water. John's descriptions are helpful in giving us a blurred picture of things, but are most helpful in showing us how futile our attempts are to imagine God. We're left with more questions than we begin with, and so we can retreat to simplicity. God's presence is, in the purest sense of the word, "good." "Good" is the white light we accept after we exhaust ourselves with colors. The most sublime truths can only be captured by simple words. After forming oceans and continents and light in the beginning, God surveyed it all and said that it was good. That's it. What else could be said? I suspect both the Lord and John would tell us that we just had to be there.

We must come to terms with the fact that we cannot know God – and yet he wants to be known by us. Can you believe that this being on the throne, surrounded by millions of intelligent, free-thinking creatures who speak of nothing but the absolute joy he brings to their lives, loves you? (After all, they say that if you really want to know someone then first see what his friends say about him.)

This is the vision that really sets Revelation up for us. Plagues and promises alike trace their origin from this God. The God who isn't named. The God who doesn't need to prove that he exists. The God who isn't too near or too far from us in this scene. He is not familiar or frightening. He doesn't move, though he moves us. In this scene, he simply is. He sits on his throne, unpainted, while all around him are swirls of music and colors and smells. It's a plain white center surrounded by an ecstasy of vibrancy. In such a way the least remarkable becomes the most interesting. This God on the throne is so far from being the subject of the painting that he paradoxically comes to dominate all other subjects.

Silent and unnamed.
Unmoved and enthroned.
Beautiful and in power.

His permanence demands an answer to the question: "This is who I am...so what are you going to do about it?"

7
Tension

I saw in the right hand of him who sat on the throne a scroll with writing on both sides and sealed with seven seals. And I saw a mighty angel proclaiming in a loud voice, "Who is worthy to break the seals and open the scroll?"

- Revelation 5.2-3

There's nothing like a good standoff in a Spaghetti Western. There's just something about that cliché scene in a dusty town where two men stand at twenty paces and face each other, fingers itching for their Peacemaker. The 'something' is in the tension; it's in that moment we wait to see who's the fastest draw. The tension is in the silence. It's in that really long second while two men with pasts stare down their future — and see who wants that future more. Mettle before metal.

Revelation chapter 5 has this tension in epic proportions. John even cries.

It turns out that all of that glorious imagery of Revelation 4 — the thrones, thunders, colors, angels, fire, rainbow, etc. — was a massive build-up to this moment. Even the bizarre way the "one who sits on the throne" is never named or really described now makes sense. All of that beauty was leading to something:

Tension.

Now we see the one sitting on the throne holding a scroll in his outstretched hand, offering it as an unspoken challenge. We know very little about the scroll, except what we can see: it has writing on both sides and is sealed with seven seals. The fact that it's sealed means that only the one with the proper permission can open it. The quest for the worthy knight begins.

A particularly strong angel bellows: "Who is worthy to break the seals and open the scroll?" It is a challenge as much as an invitation.

Heaven is silent.

All alike have never fallen, never been unkind, never selfish. They were perfect and yet not good enough to open the scroll. How can you be better than perfect? The music stops. All of the worship and sounds that roared into our imaginations now cool over into stillness. This stillness is drama of the highest kind. Everything — and I mean everything — hangs on this one question: "Who?" Is there no champion in all of the universe worthy enough to stand before the Father, take the scroll, and execute his will? There is no answer...

...and John weeps.

8
The Lamb

See, the Lion of the tribe of Judah, the Root of David, has triumphed. He is able to open the scroll and its seven seals.

- Revelation 5.5

John knows what that scroll is all about. You could tell by the way it crushed him that no one was found to open it. You could tell by the joy he felt when he discovered the only one who could.

"Who is worthy?" came the angel's booming challenge.

The only response was silence, leaving John to come to a terrifying conclusion:

What if Jesus didn't make it?

What if Jesus slipped up somewhere? What if his death wasn't enough? Where would we be? Jesus had carried all our hopes upon his back. If he couldn't do it then who could? Put yourself in John's shoes, as a man who saw his fellow disciples die, one by one, to the avarice of caesars, year after year. He had outlasted them all, only to be exiled 60 years after Jesus' death to this rock in the Aegean Sea. Was it all for nothing? Was John standing tallest among the biggest fools the world had ever known? Where had it all gone wrong?

What if the good news wasn't news at all?

What if Jesus didn't step forward? Where would you be? How would your life be different if Jesus didn't take the scroll and set out to finish the job of saving people?

All of the praise and worship fell silent at the angel's question. It's like the universe knew the weight of this moment, while earth went on unaware.

"I wept and wept," John wrote, "because no one was found who was worthy!"

Thank God the elder stepped forward when he did. "Do not weep," he consoled John. "See, the Lion of the tribe of Judah, the Root of David, has triumphed. He is able."

And then Jesus appears and the worship begins louder than ever. Everyone falls on their faces, paralyzed with joy. Just as Arthur had claimed Excalibur from its rocky sheath and thus earned the throne, so Jesus gains his throne through his sacrifice. Humanity is lost until Christ is found. It is his coronation. Now we understand why the Father upon the throne had been out of the spotlight for two chapters: this story was about Jesus' coming-of-age. Those who had praised the Father now turned their attention to the Son. He was worthy. He had done it. His sacrifice was indeed enough!

Whatever the scroll says, it seems that only Jesus is qualified to take it. If Jesus is the only one qualified to open the scroll, it must be because of his life, death, and resurrection for us. If his death for us qualifies him alone to open the scroll, then the scroll must pertain to the future salvation of humanity. That future is now in Jesus' hands.

Now, did the angel really need to ask who was worthy? No, probably not. But it made for good drama and built suspense. And when the suspense finally broke, it helped us to appreciate that Jesus' mission among us wasn't a gimme. Success was not guaranteed. There was a very real danger that he could have failed and — just for a moment — we were forced to contemplate what that would have meant for us. We were compelled to consider that we could have been slaves to sin forever, without hope or meaning. And it's only when we realize the very real risk Jesus undertook to save us that we can fully appreciate what he gained through his victory...

...power, honor, glory, wealth, strength, praise, love...

Forever.

9
The Seals

I watched as the Lamb opened the first of the seven seals. Then I heard one of the four living creatures say in a voice like thunder, "Come!"

- Revelation 6.1

Immediately after Jesus takes the scroll, he begins opening it. Jesus, it seems, is eager to conclude the work of redemption that was begun the very moment our first parents mutinied.

Or is Jesus eager at all?

Before you even arrive at questions about the four horsemen and the martyrs, you can't help but notice the sense of suffering that rudely responds to the universal acclaim of Jesus' triumph. The momentum smacks into a steel wall of reality: Despite holding the title deed to earth, Jesus isn't going to be ending this anytime soon. Neither does his assumed kingship guarantee an immediate change for the better on earth below. The four horsemen ride out: conquest, war, famine, and death. At the end of all of this, we are presented with a question in the form of the fifth seal: "How long, Jesus, are you going to let this stuff happen?" It's a question whose lease is renewed by every generation and driven many miles on roads of suffering.

Rewind. Put yourself back in John's shoes, his body rocking back and forth in hot tears as he stood before the throne. No one had stepped forward to claim humanity's future. It was over...until Jesus steps closer and claims the scroll.

But what happens when Jesus opens the scroll? A whole lot of...something? Whatever it is, it isn't a swift conclusion. Humanity has had a lot of practice waiting on God, but it's still hard.

Who would have told Eve that the promised redeemer would take some 4,000 years to arrive? When she had Cain she said, literally, "I have gotten a man; the Lord!" Did Eve think Cain was the promised Messiah? Why not?

Or why would John and the other disciples have thought that, after Jesus' death and resurrection, it would take thousands more years for him to return? "Alright! He died and conquered death with life and love. Let's go home, right?" If the first seal is opened immediately after Jesus' coronation in reaching heaven after his ascension and the sixth seal portends the signs of the end and the Second Coming, then what takes place in seals one through six narrates the events in between. It seems then that the subtext of the seals is that a lot of stuff is going to happen. The four living creatures summon the four horsemen — signaling to us that this is part of Jesus' plan to wrap up human history and fold it into a new future. This is a work in progress.

The opening of the scroll does not bring instantaneous results. We are learning again to wait. But it brings with it a comforting image: that of Jesus holding the scroll of our future. He handles our history. Sure, it takes longer than expected. Yet it also arrives sooner than we could hope.

Watch...

and pray.

10
Martyrs

I saw under the altar the souls of those who had been slain because of the word of God and the testimony they had maintained. They called out in a loud voice, "How long, Sovereign Lord, holy and true, until you judge the inhabitants of the earth and avenge our blood?"

- Revelation 6.9-10

One of the signature scenes of one of my favorite movies, *The Princess Bride,* is this great conversation between Westley and his beloved Buttercup, whose budding romance is sadly delayed by Westley's presumed death. Upon returning, he finds Buttercup resigned to marry a fool of a royal, Prince Humperdinck:

Westley: I told you I would always come for you. Why didn't you wait for me?
Buttercup: Well...you were dead.
Westley: Death cannot stop true love. All it can do is delay it for a while.
Buttercup: I will never doubt again.
Westley: There will be no need.

If you're currently fist-pumping the air, celebrating the combination of great dialog and great analog to the Christian faith, I'll wait. This is entirely appropriate – because it's there.

Okay, shall we continue?

Westley was on to something when he suggested that the best death can do is to delay love. We only need to be patient. Christ was not bothered one bit. He boasts the "keys to death and Hades." Paul was defiant when he dared Satan to respond in Romans 8: "who shall separate us from the love of Christ. . .For I am convinced that neither death nor life, neither angels or demons. . .will be able to separate us from the love of God" In light of the promise of resurrection, Paul would even go so far as to mock death:

Where, O death, is your victory?
Where, O death, is your sting?

Waiting for that reunion on the other side of death was exactly what the martyrs were told in the fifth seal of Revelation. Patience is hard in the face of unresolved justice. Someday, all of this needs to be set right, but we're more often tempted to take it into our own hands in the meantime. Yes, we know all about the final judgment and all of that, but we'd just assume lighten God's caseload by setting ourselves up as a county court and judge some of these minor cases for him. The only problem is that we're not qualified. We're not capable of fairness in deciding these things when we are both the wronged and the wrongdoers in so many other cases. We have to be like these martyrs and leave the "getting even" business up to God. For those who have suffered their share and more, that can require an awful lot of faith at times.

So we can relate to martyrs who cry out and ask God to do something about what was done to them. They're not bloodthirsty. It isn't about making sure their persecutors suffer so they can feel better. It's about justice, and all of God's promises hang upon him cleaning this all up some day. God responds by handing out white robes, which, we have seen, represents the perfect character of God. In other words, they're assured of their place in heaven. There's nothing that can jeopardize it now. There's nothing to worry about. God has a plan, and when the plan is done he'll not forget their request.

That's the really sobering thing. I've been to a number of funerals and I can't remember who most of them were for. I feel kind of guilty about that. People die, people cry, and people move on. We don't remember much about them. Walk through a cemetery sometime and realize that you don't know anything about 99.999% of the people buried there and that of all those who have graves, they probably only represent an absolute minority of all of those who have died in history. They're lost to us.

But not to God.

When Cain killed his brother Abel, God confronted Cain immediately and said, "The voice of your brother's blood calls out to me from the ground." This wasn't literal any more than these souls here are meant to be understood as literally living underneath an altar in heaven. This seal is simply meant to comfort us that these long roads of time connect us to ultimate justice. Don't worry. We'll get there even if it takes longer than you thought proper. But the real point is that God knows everyone who has died. Even if we forget, he hasn't. Abel's death called out to God, as it were, demanding justice. Our blood still cries out.

God doesn't forget.

Whatever you've suffered or had to go through in life, God hasn't forgotten. Sometimes we block away the painful memories as a way of coping. That baggage is just too heavy to keep carrying around and so we pretend it isn't there. Sometimes we have a terrible time trying to let go of what's been done to us. It's too deep. Maybe someone along the way let you down or betrayed you or stomped on your flowers or diverted your life around your dreams. The good news about the fifth seal is that God hasn't forgotten what's been done to you. It's impossible for him to forget. He can fight harder for you than you can for yourself. Don't just let him in your corner, let him in the ring. Let him box the devil for you. Let him make things right. To take justice into your own hands robs God of the privilege to defend you the way you need to be defended.

Have the faith to forgive. Forgiveness is more for you than them, anyway. It is a way of relinquishing your claims on revenge. God will surely deal with those who have hurt you, but it will be in his time. Trust him. He'll make it right. Not even death can hide your persecutors from justice, for death serves a new master and will gladly extradite all to give account of themselves to God.

Just hang in there a little while longer. You're not alone in thirsting for justice. Even if it takes a while, you will never thirst to death.

II
Black & White in
an Age of Black

The heavens receded like a scroll being rolled up, and every mountain and island was removed from its place.

Movies offer dangerous role models. I learned this as a kid when I watched a spy movie and tried to hop over the ledge of the stairs on my way out of the theater. The drop was only six feet or so, but my moment of glory was drowned out by muffled cursing as people stepped over me. Suave spy was crossed off of my "awesome occupations" list.

You can't stop us from pretending. We watch movies and read stories and play games in order to escape for a little bit. Dr. Corey Olsen, a literature professor who specializes in the fantasy of J.R.R. Tolkien, remarked:

> *Tolkien notes that any observation about escapism is usually made in a tone of scorn, but he points out that no such tone is attached to the word "escape" in normal life. Normally, escaping is a good thing, even a heroic thing. So what's the reason for this scorn? It boils down to how we view the real world. Is the real world really all there is?*

Tolkien, Olsen says, argues that "fantasy frees the mind from the bondage of drudgery and corruption" that comes with spending too much time in the world around us. The routine, the lies, the commercialism, the politics, the family feuds — it all wears us down. We need a look out the window. We need to regain the big picture of things and be reminded that life is more than paying bills and running errands.

Revelation is fantasy that is more real than reality. All of those beasts, the dragon, the horses, the creatures...they all speak to something deeper than stock markets and schedules. Revelation describes an unfamiliar future for a familiar world. We have been overburdened by familiarity with the ways of this world. Nothing seems to change. It just keeps getting worse, no matter how much we pray. It can swallow us up in hopelessness. Revelation's fantasy isn't all about the sweet waters of heaven, but about overcoming in this life. We need to get out of this rut of reality, out of believing in the permanence of skyscrapers and Tylonal. Through Revelation's fantasy, God violently rips the veil that has long separated what we see and what really is going on in this world. Behind flags we see beasts. In the chaos is a dark order; a plan for our planet disguised in randomness.

Revelation answers the question "Is the real world really all there is?" with a liberating "NO!"

There is more going on behind the scenes. We see people we call "social democrats" and "fundamentalists" and "pro-choice" and those who love the color red and people who hate mushrooms. Our world is wrapped up this way, but to focus on these things robs us of the ability to see that behind all of it is good and evil, black and white. "The game is afoot," Sherlock tells Watson. There is God...and Lucifer. Our human story really isn't about us, but them. We aren't the stars here. Nothing and no one is neutral. We must give up our safe notion of neutrality and risk a decision. Revelation shows us that the mundane matters; that all of our little choices add up to something in the end.

Revelation shows us that all of these shades of meaning and perspectives only add up to white in the end. So why continue to paint with vomited strokes of green and black — paint something that lasts!

12
Dragon in the Delivery Room, or, *A New Hope*

Then a great sign appeared in heaven: a woman clothed with the sun, and with the moon under her feet, and on her head was a crown of twelve stars. She was pregnant and was screaming in labor pains, struggling to give birth. Then another sign appeared in heaven: a huge red dragon that had seven heads and ten horns, and on its heads were seven diadem crowns. . . . The dragon stood before the woman who was about to give birth, so that he might devour her child as soon as it was born. So the woman gave birth to a son, a male child, who is going to rule over all the nations with an iron rod. Her child was suddenly caught up to God and to his throne.

- Revelation 12.1-5

By all accounts, giving birth is not at all like drinking a smoothie. It's not pleasant. Some people are in labor for a few hours, and some for what feels like months. But none of us have had a birth like the anonymous woman in Revelation 12:

> Imagine giving birth knowing that someone was standing there, waiting to kill your baby.
> Imagine that this baby is extremely important, not just to you but to the entire world.
> Imagine now that this "someone" is an enormous, red dragon.

Knowing that a wonderful new baby awaits you at the end of the tunnel of pain is a powerful psychological motivation to get through the pain. But realizing that as soon as you give birth your baby is going to be killed...that's too much. That's inhumane. That's the devil.

The dragon attacks the woman when she is most vulnerable. That's the way the devil works. He waits behind corners. He comes up from behind. But God is committed to the helpless; to those who cannot possibly defend themselves, both mother and child. Jesus defended Mary, telling Martha that Mary had made the better choice. He shielded Mary again as she anointed his feet, telling the men to leave her alone. He protected the children from the disciples, telling them that children should never been turned away from him.

This great, red, Middle-Eastern dragon that attacks the helpless isn't the medieval, European dragon of our imagination. He's a winged serpent, an Asian cousin to the Chinese dragon. Isaiah 27.1 describes this dragon in a familiar way:

> *The Lord will punish with his sword—his fierce, great and powerful sword—Leviathan the gliding serpent, Leviathan the coiling serpent.*

In the Greek version of the Old Testament, the word for serpent here is *drakonta*, the same word used here in Revelation for "dragon." This is the Garden of Eden: Part Two, where Jesus stands where Adam fell. Back there, the serpent/dragon attacked a woman and won. So a child was promised to Eve who would destroy the serpent. Now that child has arrived, and both he and this woman escape the dragon. The message is alive with hope, as Revelation 12 reacquaints us with the devil's colossal failure to destroy Jesus and so fails to influence the future of mankind. Jesus was the boy who lived where Adam died, and because he lived we will live. Revelation 12 depicts the devil's constant failures, past, present, and future. This is a reality at odds with our own, because we often see the devil as winning (or at least not losing) in the world around us. But Revelation shows us a dragon that laughably (though he should not be laughed at) cannot help but fail to thwart God's plans for his people.

The devil is a loser but not a quitter. We're told to beware "because the devil has gone down to you! He is filled with fury because he knows his time is short" (v. 12). His clock is ticking. Remember that no matter how much you feel like the devil is chasing you and harassing you, his time is short. The woman runs, but that doesn't mean she's losing. You should expect his attention, but you should also know that Jesus has made a way of escape. Naturally, some of us would like to take up the sword and try our hand at dragon-slayer (apologies to St. George). It's not meant to be for one simple reason: you don't have to fight the devil because he is already defeated. To fight back against the devil is to act as if God hasn't vanquished him. This is why Revelation focuses hanging on, enduring, and withstanding the fury of the foe. It's the greatest statement of faith when you don't feel threatened by the devil. You go on following God, ignoring the storm raging around you. You ignore his threats, because it's just his lame attempt to convince you of his relevance when you know the truth: the universe is so over him.

Jesus wins. I'm with him. I don't have time for losers.

13
The Dragon Strikes Back

The dragon stood on the shore of the sea. And I saw a beast coming out of the sea. It had ten horns and seven heads, with ten crowns on its horns, and on each head a blasphemous name. The beast I saw resembled a leopard, but had feet like those of a bear and a mouth like that of a lion. The dragon gave the beast his power and his throne and great authority. One of the heads of the beast seemed to have had a fatal wound, but the fatal wound had been healed. The whole world was filled with wonder and followed the beast. People worshiped the dragon because he had given authority to the beast, and they also worshiped the beast and asked, "Who is like the beast? Who can wage war against it?"

- Revelation 13.1-4

The dragon may have failed to kill the child and his mother, but it wasn't long before he went after her remaining children (12.17). This refers to all of Jesus' true followers down through the ages. To accomplish this, the dragon calls up his gang: the beast from the sea and the beast from the land. Each beast has a particular set of skills. Sea Beast is about brute force. He will beat you up unless you worship the dragon. Land Beast doesn't mind throwing a few punches, but he'd rather trick you into following the dragon. He's an inside guy.

The dragon has had a lot of time to realize that many humans successfully resist one of these approaches, but seldom both. Outward persecution can summon up a spirit of courage and defiance in some, like those who hid the Jews in Nazi Europe. Inward corruption can provoke the same spirit, as it did in Martin Luther when he refused to make deposits of faith in the spiritual bankruptcy of the church in his day. To resist both requires a living, flourishing relationship with God.

Such prophecies fill people with fear. It's terrifying to think that God could permit this when the devil is supposedly defeated. But consider this: by giving us Revelation 13, God has laid open for us the devil's playbook. We *know* what he's going to do. We *know* what his strategy is. We even *know* what we must do to be prepared. Why should we be afraid?

In the American Civil War, Confederate General Robert E. Lee knew that a long war ultimately favored the North, so he drew up plans to invade quickly and decisively. He outlined it all in Special Orders 191, a two-page plan that he sent to his commanders. One commander famously wadded up the orders and chewed them like tobacco after reading them. But someone else ended up using the paper to wrap some cigars. These cigars — and the plans — were discovered by the Union army as it shadowed Lee. The result was the Battle of Antietam, the most important battle in the war and the one that decided the future of the entire nation. It was the bloodiest 12 hours on American soil, leaving 23,000 Americans dead in a Union victory that turned the tide at last (though no one knew it at the time). Before Antietam, England and France were considering recognizing the Confederacy as an independent nation and raising the chances of the South's victory. Afterwards, there was no looking back.

Friends, we have the battle plans. We know what the dragon is going to try and do. Our God is so powerful that nothing is a secret from him. He can reach into the enemy's camp at will and show his soldiers from which direction they will be attacked. Readers of Revelation cannot possibly be caught off-guard. What more could our Father possibly do for us? Listen carefully to his voice until you know it by heart. Follow his plans for you carefully. He is the general in charge and will not lead us astray. Why should the enemy's plans frighten us? The fact that they are laid out for us in Revelation should only confirm our confidence in our Commander.

14
Return of the Jesus

I looked, and there before me was a white cloud, and seated on the cloud was one like a son of man with a crown of gold on his head and a sharp sickle in his hand. Then another angel came out of the temple and called in a loud voice to him who was sitting on the cloud, "Take your sickle and reap, because the time to reap has come, for the harvest of the earth is ripe." So he who was seated on the cloud swung his sickle over the earth, and the earth was harvested.

- Revelation 14.14-16

Jesus is coming again.

We can learn a lot about ourselves by how we respond to that statement. Name that emotion. Put your finger on it. Is it fear? Resignation? Excitement? Dread? Often, it's more complicated than a single emotion. Sure, if push came to shove we'd love for Jesus to come. But while he delays — let's be honest — we find there are many things we'd like to do. Deep inside, many of us want Jesus to come...when it's convenient for us. In this way we treat Jesus like he's our ride from the mall. We don't want to be forced to wait for him, but neither do we want him to arrive before we're finished shopping.

When we get older, we find we care about the mall of life less and less. Suddenly, we cannot understand why the younger people aren't more excited about Jesus coming back. Surely it's a sign of the age we live in. We view the Second Coming as the solution to our problems. Only Jesus can fix your bad liver or turn the hearts of your children back to him. We're done shopping, and we cannot understand why others aren't done, too. All we've really done over the years is dress our selfishness as piety.

This isn't to say we don't have any real desire to see Jesus. We do. But we have to recognize and be disgusted by the amount of selfishness in our spiritual desires. Regardless of how you feel or pretend to feel about the Second Coming, Revelation portrays it as an event of undiminished hope for his followers and utter terror for his enemies.

John records the reaction of the wicked in the events foretold under the sixth seal: "They called to the mountains and the rocks, 'Fall on us and hide us from the face of him who sits on the throne and from the wrath of the Lamb! For the great day of their wrath has come, and who can withstand it?" (Rev. 6.16). There must be no rejoicing that the wicked will one day "get their due." No, all who will have been saved will have been saved by a thread of grace. The terror of the lost is the terror of someone watching from shore as the last boat evacuates people from a burning city. It's hopeless. It's tragic. It's a moment of supreme spiritual clarity. It's too late.

We see the contrast of reactions to the Second Coming in Revelation 19. There heaven exults over Babylon's fall and the return of Christ. A "voice like a great multitude" shouts from heaven: "Let us rejoice and be glad and give him glory! For the wedding of the Lamb has come, and his bride has made herself ready." From the point of view of God's followers, the Second Coming is a reunion. Better still, it is the moment when the groom has finally learned that the bride is ready for the wedding and comes to pick her up so that they might go and be married. What could be better than your wedding day?

The mood of chapter 19 turns darker when the lost are in view. Jesus is seen as a warrior on a white horse who tramples his enemies in bloody conquest. An angel ominously calls it "the great supper of God." It's not a heroic, last-second victory. It's a massacre. There is no contest. Jesus wins.

> On this mountain he will destroy the shroud that enfolds all peoples, the sheet that covers all nations; he will swallow up death forever. The Sovereign Lord will wipe away the tears from all faces; he will remove his people's disgrace from all the earth. The Lord has spoken. In that day they will say, "Surely this is our God; we trusted in him, and he saved us. This is the Lord, we trusted in him; let us rejoice and be glad in his salvation."
> - Isaiah 25.7-9

15
Beastly Power

One of the heads of the beast seemed to have had a fatal wound, but the fatal wound had been healed. The whole world was filled with wonder and followed the beast. People worshiped the dragon because he had given authority to the beast, and they also worshiped the beast and asked, "Who is like the beast? Who can wage war against it?"

- Revelation 14.14-16

In some way the Sea Beast is dealt a mortal wound. Everyone thinks he is going to die, but miraculously survives. We would call this a sort of resurrection. And it's this half-hearted resurrection that fills the whole world with wonder: "Who can take on the beast? Look at all the power it has! It's invincible!"

We respect power. We understand power through physical violence, economic force, social pressure, and even religious coercion. We complain about people in power, but power means control. If I get power in some way, I can have control over my own life. Humans want control. This is why the devil's strategy in Revelation 13 isn't that surprising to us. It's smart. It's also why God's strategy is foreign to us: Three angels that just fly around and warn us? What good does that do?

Whether we would like to admit it or not, the dragon's ways are more familiar to us. They are the ways of our natural selves. We can understand how many could lose their faith in God in a world that seems completely under the dragon's control because we are innately conditioned to respect the emblems of such power. It's a language we speak fluently.

It is the power of love — God's love — that we distrust. We have been told that such love is weakness. We see the principled men following Gandhi, sitting before British tanks and fear for them. We see a mother giving birth to a baby before a hungry dragon and fear for her. But when you see things from God's perspective, you are forced to realize that love always wins in the end. We must have confidence in love as power beyond power; love is the antidote to power. Or, if we must press on, it isn't power that's hoarded, but generously tithed to those around us. Power is, like static electricity, dangerous when it exists only within ourselves. It must be discharged through materials capable of receiving it.

Nowhere is this clearer than at the cross. At the cross we see the power of the dragon and the power of love collide. Jesus was beaten, screamed at, mocked, lied to, misrepresented, betrayed, and rejected. These tactics would defeat most anyone. These are the tactics that seek a reply in kind from us. We give insult for insult and blow for blow. That is the language of the world.

Jesus' restraining love wasn't weakness. In fact, it terrified his accusers. Pilate, feeling insecure that nothing he could do could penetrate Jesus, boasted: "Don't you realize I have power either to free you or to crucify you?" (John 19.10). It is a sign of weakness to have to remind someone of the power you hold over them. Jesus finally responded: "You would have no power over me if it were not given to you from above" (John 19.11). Crowds are wreathed in rage, almost possessed and definitely blood-thirsty. Veteran, grizzled Roman soldiers stand by, restless for violence. The governor taunts Jesus, dangling a cross in front of him. Weakness is dripping from this scene; at least, from everywhere *but* Jesus.

> It drips from the mob that lost control of themselves.
> It drips from the religious leaders who felt powerless to kill Jesus themselves.
> It drips from Pilate when he feels he needs to remind Jesus of his power.

The fact that Jesus endures this situation calmly is frightening. The storm beat against him hard and he didn't even flinch.

That's because he knew that the power in this world ultimately belongs to God. We must remember that no boss or king or president has ultimate power. We simply must remember that there is a God higher than the beasts and the dragon. We must learn the language of love to gain the only kind of power that matters. Only then can we endure the hot, threatening breath of the beasts. Their power is weakness.

16
Babylon

*Then one of the seven angels who had the seven bowls came and spoke to me.
"Come," he said, "I will show you the condemnation and punishment of the great
prostitute who sits on many waters, with whom the kings of the earth committed
sexual immorality and the earth's inhabitants got drunk with the wine of her
immorality." So he carried me away in the Spirit to a wilderness, and there I saw
a woman sitting on a scarlet beast that was full of blasphemous names and had
seven heads and ten horns.*

- Revelation 17.1-3

This is Babylon. John "saw that the woman was drunk with the blood of God's people,
the blood of those who bore testimony to Jesus" (Rev. 17.6). She enjoys massacring
God's people. She's intoxicated by violence. She's a vampire.

The beast she rides is almost identical to the Sea Beast of Rev. 13, that great persecuting
power the dragon sent after the rest of the good woman's children. This woman is
gaudily adorned like a Christmas tree with purple and scarlet and gold and gems and
pearls. It's not the woman's jewelry that is a problem, but the fact that she is dressed
to seduce. The good woman of Revelation 12 is adorned with the sun (an ode to the
radiant, undiscovered nudity of Eden) and wears a golden crown called *stephanos* in
Greek — a crown of victory.

When you compare the two women, you cannot help but bet that it's the wicked
woman who wins. She's the one riding this terrifying beast which just stomps all over
God's people while she drinks their blood. We recognize her. She's distinctly Roman in
character. Smash. Crush. Destroy. By comparison, the "good" woman of chapter twelve
just seems to barely survive. Raise your hand if you want to join the side that barely
seems to survive? Man, we know this Babylon chick is rough, but she's the type we find
attractive. Maybe she's on the wrong team, but we get her style. That's how people get
ahead around here.

Once again, we've got it all upside down.

The angel draws our attention to Babylon in order to "show you the condemnation and punishment of the great prostitute." At the pinnacle of this world's success, we are reminded of its ruin. The "kings of the earth" she has seduced into sin reign over the realms that now belong to our God: "The kingdoms of this world have become the kingdoms of our Lord and of His Christ, and He shall reign forever and ever!" (Rev. 11.15). "Fallen! Fallen is Babylon the Great!" another angel announces. "Come out of her, my people, so that you will not share in her sins, so that you will not receive any of her plagues. . . .for her sins are piled up to heaven, and God has remembered her crimes" (Rev. 18.2, 4-5).

We are reassured of her judgment, which is a byproduct of God's ultimate justice. The world's winning streaks have strings attached because the world is tethered to failure. Let them boast. Let them revel in their apparent success. They may count their victories, not knowing that every little victory they steal just makes Christ's ultimate victory all the more impressive. "Give back to her as she has given; pay her back double for what she has done. . . Give her as much torment and grief as the glory and luxury she gave herself" (Rev. 18.6-7). Babylon, that power that puts a pretty face on all the dragon's doings, will some day pay for the families she has broken, for the blood of God's people she has thirsted for.

So when she rampages through the world, when she points to the concrete skyscrapers that rise like a modern Babel, it is at this point — this moment when she looks the most terrifying and beautiful — that we are to remember that she is judged and fallen. We are told that behind this projection of strength and attraction is emptiness and ugliness. As she rises to her full height, we are to remember she's fallen.

Mene, Mene, Tekel.

17
Judgment Day

Then I saw a large white throne and the one who was seated on it; the earth and the heaven fled from his presence, and no place was found for them. And I saw the dead, the great and the small, standing before the throne. Then books were opened, and another book was opened—the book of life. So the dead were judged by what was written in the books, according to their deeds. The sea gave up the dead that were in it, and Death and Hades gave up the dead that were in them, and each one was judged according to his deeds.

- Revelation 20.11-13

So your friend said she has to go to court this afternoon and if you're like me you'll ask: "What did you do this time?" Court is kind of a bad word. When we tell our boss that we need some time off to go to court, it usually precedes this clumsy waterfall of an explanation: "But, uh, it's not really my fault" or maybe "I just messed up a little." We are guilty by association.

Tell that to Sojourner Truth. Upon being freed from slavery with her infant, she set out to find a lawyer who could free her five year old son, Peter. As New York's emancipation law was about to be enacted, many slave-owners quickly sold their slaves to Southern states to make money off of them while they still could. Such was Peter's fate. The lawyer asked for $5, which Sojourner obtained from some Quakers by walking 12 miles. Months passed, and Sojourner learned how her son had been traded around Alabama and abused terribly. (One of his masters would later hit his own wife so hard she would die.) Finally, she secured his release and he came back home. Sojourner saw the justice system as her friend in having the power to hear her plea and give her justice.

It is because human courts are so unreliable in their justice that we have tended to look upon God's courts with the same distrust. We are afraid that perhaps we haven't confessed enough of our sins, or lived well enough. At the very least, we don't like the idea of our lives being scrutinized by some divine spy agency, and so we head in one of two directions: either we magnify our fear of the judgment, or we try to plaster it over with talk of grace. Both reactions are due to fear, though one sounds holier while the other is more honest.

The truth is that this final judgment scene is good news for God's people, because Revelation is fundamentally about how God brings justice into an unjust world. What was done to Jesus and his followers was deeply wrong. What the dragons and beasts and wicked woman do seem to us to break something that cannot be fixed. It is a poison to the very atmosphere of God's moral universe. Something must be done about it, and Revelation was gifted to us to help us see what exactly God plans to do about evil and injustice. What we find in Revelation is that God doesn't fly off the handle and just nuke the world as some believe. We see a carefully controlled courtroom with three phases: investigation, sentencing, and execution. The deepest depths of the sea could not hide people from the day of judgment. It doesn't matter how "untouchable" your persecutors may seem to be now. Some day they will meet your heavenly Father, who will vindicate you. This judgment is the answer to the cry of the martyrs, who beg God to take action in the same way Abel's blood demanded it (Genesis 4.10). Satan must pay for sin in the end, for the ruin he has wrought by his rebellion.

For God's people, the judgment is a day of great hope and longing. It's when our salvation is at last realized, and sin is finally seen for what it is. It will no longer be able to hide behind a suit and tie. It must be exposed to the light. It must be named. God's judgment is precisely the reason you must not take justice into your own hands. Leave it to him. Trust it to him.

> *The heavens will disappear with a roar; the elements will be destroyed by fire, and the earth and everything done in it will be laid bare. Since everything will be destroyed in this way, what kind of people ought you to be?*

Peter looks forward to this judgment and asks the question that really sits before us, purring like a kitten waiting for you to pet it:

> If *that*,
> now *what?*

18
Hell is Love

Then Death and Hades were thrown into the lake of fire. This is the second death—the lake of fire. If anyone's name was not found written in the book of life, that person was thrown into the lake of fire.

- Revelation 20.14-15

The cruelest, coldest words one human being can say to another is "go to Hell!" The fact that most people mean it rather flippantly only compounds the criminality of such a thought. I should think that it would go better for a man to say those words and fully mean them, than to toss them out like a grenade while insisting you didn't mean to hurt anyone.

Hell is described as a lake of fire in Revelation. *Where* Hell is tells us a lot about *what* it is. After the New Jerusalem descends out of heaven, the wicked are resurrected and besiege God's city. (It's like God drew them into the siege — what an easy way to get them to show up to court!) That's as far as they get before God presides over the judgment, which is meant to convince the guilty of their guilt by showing them that they rebuffed his constant love. Judgment finished, fire streams from the throne of God, burning up all that can be burned. It is in this fire that Hell (briefly) exists. What we learn about Hell here goes against so much of what we've been taught.

First, Hell exists outside of the City of God. Those who are in Hell are separated from God, from fellowship with his friends, and from the ministry of the angels. Hell is separation from God.

Second, Hell is temporary. God's objection has been to get rid of the weed of sin, not people. The only people who perish are those who insist on clinging on to it. There is no need to burn them forever and torture them. He only wishes to destroy sin and remake the world as it was meant to be.

Third, Hell is love. Those who have chosen the dragon's side have essentially voted to live in a world where God doesn't exist. They wish to be completely free from him. But there is no *universe* where God doesn't exist. You cannot live without God. His fingerprint is on every person he formed with his own hands; his breath is our very soul. To reject his presence is to reject all presence. Hell is a place where a God of love gives those who don't choose him what they want. C.S. Lewis echoed this through his Ransom character when he wrote that "a man can't be taken to hell, or sent to hell: you can only get there on your own steam." Lewis added elsewhere: "I willingly believe that the damned are, in one sense, successful, rebels to the end; that the doors of hell are locked on the inside."

Hell is on the other side of the coin from the cross. There is no more terrifying example of how far the love of God will go for the sake of you and I. It is a strange thing that shall never lose its strangeness after eons have passed in the heavenly country. Our minds constantly scratch the walls for reason: "Why would people choose it? Why should it have to happen?" But how the love of God attends he who hates him most! Take pity then on those who take that exit. Though some may be snarly and nasty, they deserve all the sympathetic love we can offer.

Hell is not terrible because of the physical suffering so much as for the eternal separation from God and thus from his love and from his life. How twisted the soul must grow as it shrinks toward Hell; how warped the heart that it should come to believe Satan's lies and follow him down that rocky road. God is the one who makes it rocky. It's hard to get to Hell.

19
Rest & Restlessness

And the smoke of their torment will rise for ever and ever. There will be no rest day or night for those who worship the beast and its image, or for anyone who receives the mark of its name....Then I heard a voice from heaven say, Write this: Blessed are the dead who die in the Lord from now on. "Yes," says the Spirit, "they will rest from their labor, for their deeds will follow them."

- Revelation 14.11, 13

In these verses we see an interesting contrast between the saved and lost: rest. It's a story of the haves and the have-nots. Isaiah chips in when he attests that "there is no peace . . . for the wicked" (Isaiah 48.22) and "the wicked are like the tossing sea, which cannot rest" (Isaiah 57.20). The immediate context of verse 13 concerns those who give their lives for the Lord, but they are praised precisely because they're able to find rest, while the wicked are not. The rest in death that the righteous find is in some way a type of the rest we will all find in God's heavenly realm. The Spirit is eager to congratulate them! They've made it to the doorstep!

This ability to find rest at last is the hope of the Christian. Jesus beckons us towards finding this rest in him: "Come to me, all you who are weary and burdened, and I will give you rest. Take my yoke upon you and learn from me, for I am gentle and humble in heart, and you will find rest for your souls" (Matt. 11.28-29). In contrast, when Cain murdered his brother Abel, he realized that his destiny in sin was to "be a restless wanderer on the earth" (Gen. 4.14).

The Sabbath [lit. "rest"] holiday that God gave to his people was itself a rest in remembrance of God's creative rest on the seventh day of Creation week (Gen. 2.2-3; Ex. 20.8-11). The Sabbath is a rest in time, while the Promised Land was to be a rest in space. That is, the Sabbath is a type of heavenly eternity while the land was a type of heavenly space. In recounting Israel's rebellion, God says that because Israel did not enter his rest, the promise still remains. The author of Hebrews urges us to "make every effort to enter that rest, so that no one will perish by following their example of disobedience" (Heb. 4.11). Modern men and women stand at the borders of the Promised Land, and we must make the choice to enter or to wander as Israel once did. Inside this land we will find rest for our souls because it is the land of our Prince, Jesus.

To remain outside of this rest is restlessness.

It is not our place to judge a person's eternal fate — we give that to God — but you can get a sense of the direction you are heading by whether your life is characterized by increasing restlessness or restfulness. This isn't to say that if you can't sleep or if a bunch of things go wrong in Job-like glory that you are lost. We are talking about the state of your soul, not just your body. Even amidst the storms of stress that Job suffered, he had peace and trust in God: "Naked I came from my mother's womb, and naked I will depart. The Lord gave and the Lord has taken away. May the name of the Lord be praised" (Job 1.20).

Accept the rest Jesus offers you today. Relax in him every chance you can get, and when the storms come you will find peace. Feelings of peace and safety are born along the gentle waves of rest. If ever you have a chance to cease one day from the sin struggle, then it is by siding with Jesus. He offers us a future, eternal rest in a New Promised Land. Hug that promise today and begin living with rest in mind.

20
The Healing Havens

Then the angel showed me the river of the water of life, as clear as crystal, flowing from the throne of God and of the Lamb down the middle of the great street of the city. On each side of the river stood the tree of life, bearing twelve crops of fruit, yielding its fruit every month. And the leaves of the tree are for the healing of the nations.

- Revelation 22.1-2

Somehow it has crept into our minds that heaven is this static, stagnant place. It's the place with the angels and the harps and all of that. It doesn't seem like a place to grow and learn, let alone heal. Yet it's there. The thing we call sin has done lasting damage, the kind that even God cannot heal in an instant. Heaven is rehab.

The centerpiece of this painting is a river that flows from the throne of God, the Source of all life. This water gives life also to the tree of life, which has roots on both banks. The Garden of Eden has been restored to this new earth. It was this tree that Adam and Eve ate from and it was this tree that they were banned from eating ever again in Genesis 3.22-24:

The Lord God said, "The man has now become like one of us, knowing good and evil. He must not be allowed to reach out his hand and take also from the tree of life and eat, and live forever." So the Lord God banished him from the Garden of Eden to work the ground from which he had been taken. After he drove the man out, he placed on the east side of the Garden of Eden cherubim and a flaming sword flashing back and forth to guard the way to the tree of life.

God was adamant that the way to the tree be guarded by an angel with a lightsaber, lest our fallen first parents eat from the tree again and live forever as sinners. This tree is potent. Now the danger is past and we see that the tree — and eternal life — is restored to God's people. We don't innately possess immortality any more than a battery possesses infinite energy. We've been separated from the source, and we need to recharge down here through things like sleep and recreation and Sabbath. The fruit gives eternal life because the tree has life. The tree has life because it is watered by the river of life. The river has life because it comes from the throne of God, "who alone has immortality" (2 Timothy 3.16). God is the source of all the living that we do.

The healing of the nations is also community building. The nations of the world have never been united, yet this is how it's done. While wall-breaking between disconnected communities should be part of our passion as Christians, we must recognize that global unity is only possible in the presence of the only being that unites all people: the Father of all nations.

Dante wrote that the path to this new Eden passes through two rivers: Lethe and Eunoe. Lethe is the river of forgetfulness where we drink to forget the terrors of life in the old times. Drinking from Eunoe strengthens our memory of good things. I think what Dante gets right is that he emphasizes that our memories need healing as well as our bodies. This is hard work. God can't just reinstall his operating system in our minds, wiping it clean and starting over. How then can we be healed?

The first step is rescue. We need to be removed from this place and airlifted somewhere safe. The second step is judgment. Judgment dredges up all of the garbage of our lives so we can witness Jesus forgive it all. Judgment is the gift of a clear conscience. But then Revelation 20 talks about this kind of judgment where we get to go through the records of life to gain some closure to our lingering questions. Third, we see the execution of our tormentor, Satan. Thus we are assured that "oppression will not rise up a second time" (Nahum 1.9, HCSB). We are safe. Finally, we are nourished by this tree of life, standing in the healing presence of God. The word for "healing" is *therateuein*, which can mean things like "to care for the sick," "to treat medically," or "to cure." The leaves — a common ingredient in natural healing practices — receive their power from God. Only a continued communion with God can heal our sin-scarred souls, and a bigger dose than we get now.

You have been wounded by the world we live in. Our condition has been stabilized by our faith in the cross of Christ, but we are still desperately malnourished. We are weak and battered and frail and in the deepest places of our being terribly exhausted. But there is healing, friend. There is restoration and awakening to complete healthiness - physically, spiritually, emotionally, and psychologically. Our medicine is both fruit and leaf — food and medicine — as our Physician brings us back to where we were meant to be.

As Frodo concluded his adventure in Middle-Earth, he stood on the shore of the Grey Havens. He had saved the world, and came to wish his other friends goodbye as they took their one-way trip to heavenly Valinor. Surprising his friends, Frodo took his spot on the ship. His home had been saved, he said, but not for him. His wounds required medicine from a different world. I think that's true for some of us as well.

21
Love is a Plague

I saw in heaven another great and marvelous sign: seven angels with the seven last plagues—last, because with them God's wrath is completed. And I saw what looked like a sea of glass glowing with fire and, standing beside the sea, those who had been victorious over the beast and its image and over the number of its name. They held harps given them by God.

- Revelation 15.1-2

People have often held God to a double-standard when it comes to the seven last plagues. We want him to save us from our troublesome boss or from the disappointment of loss, but when we read about the seven last plagues we sort of switch allegiances and sympathize with the defenseless masses being annihilated by God's temper tantrum.

In the fourth plague, we read that the people "were seared by the intense heat and they cursed the name of God, who had control over these plagues, but they refused to repent and glorify him" (v. 9). We might naturally think, "Yeah, well, I would refuse to glorify someone who was scorching me with fire, too." But that attitude misses the context. We want God to give us justice and peace from our sin-led tormentors. We are not far behind David when he cries out in Psalm 109: *"May his descendants be cut off, their names blotted out from the next generation. May the iniquity of his fathers be remembered before the Lord; may the sin of his mother never be blotted out. May their sins always remain before the Lord, that he may blot out their name from the earth."* After all that David had gone through — the rebellion by his son and the persecution for over a decade by King Saul — we are cheering for him. We want to see his worthless enemies destroyed. And yet when we witness God doing so in the context of these plagues, we suddenly are horrified, as if God is committing genocide against the human race.

We need to take a step back and remember a few things: **First**, that only those who have completely rejected God are the objects of the plagues. These are not the fence-sitters, but people who have made their final choice in rejecting God. God doesn't harm innocents. **Second**, we must remember that when the plagues fell on Egypt before the Exodus they were used to release God's people from the grip of their tormentors. These plagues are not simply punitive, but salvific in nature. **Third**, the reaction of the wicked (refusing to repent) is indicative to the entire universe that all who could be saved have been saved. Everyone has made their choice, either for God or against him.

One cannot sugarcoat these plagues as if they're something pleasant. They're not. They may be metaphorical in one sense or another, but they do have a serious effect in the real world. They serve as the divine hand forcibly peeling back the tightened fingers of Satan's followers from the throat of God's people. The plagues are an expression of God's love for his people. It's the message of the cross applied. On that hill we saw how far God will go to save people, while in this valley we see him exercising this wordless love. He will not allow his people to perish from the earth. He will superheat the sun and supercharge the sky if that's what it takes to keep you safe.

The plagues are painful to those who have made the conscious choice to reject the life that God offers. Suffering is the language of sin. Though it has been so frequently translated by God into blessings for us, it is not native to his creation. It is fair that those who have inflicted so much suffering on the world should themselves suffer; not for the sake of suffering, but so that it can be plain to all that all who would accept love have. It is fair to save people from the tyranny of sin. God has given sin more than enough time to play out its hand. We see the face of sin for what it is, for it kisses with a tongue of flame.

We must not be callous in discussing these plagues. This is a place where the head can get in the way of the heart. Those are real, tragic people there in the creases of Revelation. They are God's fallen sons. They are my lost sisters strangely estranged. They are people without hope and so without future. If pain is the language of the lost, then it is God's only way of getting through to them. They would not listen to love in any other tone.

22
Certain Uncertainty

Woe! Woe! Woe to the inhabitants of the earth, because of the trumpet blasts about to be sounded by the other three angels!

- Revelation 8.13

We must beware of our tendency to be addicted to certainty. Some of us freak out when the existential chaos of the unknown is introduced. We like life neat and in order, thank you very much! This need for certainty is really just a need for control, and Revelation defies such a need.

You have likely met folks who are so fiercely dogmatic about their view of Revelation that anyone who doesn't agree lacks firm faith. "Do not waiver, brother or sister, this is what the truth is!" Maybe you have doubts as to their interpretation but, hey, you don't have a better idea so you might as well go along with it. You are so convinced that what they say is right, but when you walk away you realize you can't remember why it was right, only that the speaker was just so certain and so confident in what they're saying. Confidence is contagious.

But confidence doesn't mean someone is right. Sometimes, it can be a weakness.

For instance, we must treat the Land Beast of Revelation 13 with special care. Its great talent is deception, after all, and gobbling up over-simplifying, over-confident believers seems a real possibility. We must do the hard work of prayerfully interpreting Scripture, comparing text with text, until we have some sense of its meaning. We should not shy away from this challenge merely because it's difficult. We must give up any feeling of entitlement to spiritual success without work. We should find an interpretation that seems to align with the evidence, but we must leave a little room for self-doubt. Perhaps God will change our mind in the future? Where God is less clear, we should be less clear.

We cannot deliver an ultimatum to the Book of Revelation: "Give us your secrets or I won't give you my time!" Of course, people seldom put it like that. Rather, they conclude the book is too hard, too vague, too impolitic for polite company. That is our polite way of losing faith. "Matthew, Mark, Luke, and John are enough!" we might say. (Of course, there is the fact that John wrote Revelation...)

This isn't to suggest that we shouldn't be digging deeply in Revelation, but that there is something in many of us that *needs* to know. And so we settle on our interpretations of every tiny thing, and never give a thought to any weaknesses such a position may hold. "Our church fathers thought this way!" we may declare in our defense. That is not enough.

If you are absolutely certain that the Land Beast of Revelation 13 is, for example, some group in India, then you are going to be looking in that direction. The Land Beast excels at nothing if not deception, and so if you're wrong then there's a chance you'll never see it coming. Getting Revelation right is about questioning ourselves. We need some spiritual checkups every so often. We need to allow our beliefs to be tested and updated when needed. On what God has so plainly revealed, be as unshakeable as an oak in the rain. In those things that require deep contemplation, be humble and careful.

Certainty is not a virtue.

23
The Holy City

I saw the Holy City, the new Jerusalem, coming down out of heaven from God, prepared as a bride beautifully dressed for her husband. And I heard a loud voice from the throne saying, "Look! God's dwelling place is now among the people, and he will dwell with them.

- Revelation 21.2-3

The ancient Jews used to speak of *Yerushalayim shel malah*, the spiritual Jerusalem in heaven that the earthly Jerusalem simply dreams of becoming. Rabbi Israel Goldstein once wrote that this "'higher Jerusalem' is an unattainable goal, yet it must remain an indispensable objective."

Revelation isn't content with simply dreaming. In Revelation, the New Jerusalem is delivered to earth. God's capital city — the place of his eternal presence — comes to us. It's God's final act of glorious condescension. First, God visited Adam and Eve in the cool of the day of the garden to bring caution and comfort to his erring ones. Then God came in the person of Jesus, in the past as a baby to die for us and in the promise as our king. But it does not end there. It culminates with the city and the joyous announcement: "Look! God's dwelling place is now among the people, and he will dwell with them" (Revelation 21.3). God has come down to man once more, never to leave! It's not another visit by a foreign dignitary. God is moving. The New Jerusalem is him moving his house down to your (but really his) yard. No more goodbyes.

The New Jerusalem is more than just a city. It represents God's presence being permanently planted in our midst. It is what the temple ultimately aspired to be. Jesus fulfilled the sacrifices, but the promise of his presence remains unfulfilled until this moment. It is not the fulfillment of a few prophecies, but the ultimate realization of everything God has aimed for.

The New Jerusalem is more than just a city. It's more than just additional space. We make a big deal about how big it is (about 1500 miles by 1500 miles by 1500 miles high). Estimates have been made as to how many billions of people could live in such a city (with 12 ft ceilings, someone on YouTube did the math to suggest that if split into cake layers, the New Jerusalem could cover the entire earth — 89 floors high!). It's fun to think on, but it really is beside the point, which is that there is plenty of room for you in God's city. You are welcome there. The city is for you. It is home.

The New Jerusalem is more than just a city. Cities in the ancient world were where you went to be safe when enemies attacked. The New Jerusalem isn't just a place but represents a coming age of absolute physical, emotional, and spiritual safety. There's no more looking before crossing the street.

No more worrying about your children when you lose sight of them. No more worrying about what teachers might be telling your kids. No more suspicion that someone might be lying to you.

Yes, it's beautiful. But the beauty is deeper than the gold and pearls and square footage. The beauty is in the fact that God himself will live among us. It's been God's dream all along. In the beginning he walked with us in Eden. After sin, he had humans build a sanctuary "that I may dwell among you." In the New Jerusalem, God's great goal is finally realized. He is with us! And where he is, we finally arrive at the fullest sense of the word "home."

24
All Things New and Novel

Then I saw a new heaven and a new earth, for the first heaven and the first earth had passed away, and there was no longer any sea.

- Revelation 21.1

"Ahhhh," said *How I Met Your Mother's* Barney, building up to his point: "But 'new is always better' is my oldest rule, which makes it the best!" Barney, played by the ridiculously talented Neil Patrick Harris, fingers the modern "new is best" axiom that is so clearly seen with technology. Late night comedians make jokes about iPhones and computers being considered obsolete shortly after launch. CNET editor Roger Cheng openly complained after an iPad he bought seven months prior was replaced with a new model. "Apple," he whined, "I thought we had a deal. I buy one of your products, and I'm guaranteed roughly a year feeling like I've got the latest and greatest Apple has to offer." He said he was "shocked" and "a little annoyed" to find that Apple released an even better version of his product half a year later. "Thanks for making my 'new iPad' obsolete," he griped.

What's up with this? The guy's six-month-old iPad wasn't any less wonderful or capable after the newer version was released. It worked just the same. What changed? Cheng said it himself: the "feeling like I've got the latest and greatest" is gone. We chase that feeling of newness because new is better. We seldom even question it (though those who upgraded from Windows XP to Vista discovered it's not always true). Not to oversimplify it, but we haven't always lived in an age where new was best. In some ages, "new" was handled with suspicion. Old worked. Old could be trusted. Old was respected. "New" had to prove itself. Today, it is the other way around: old stuff has to prove why it's worth keeping around. (I'm looking at you, last year's shoes!)

Revelation is the intersection of both old and new. The "new earth" it speaks of is not new in the way we appraise the word. No one who lusts for the new heavens and the new earth merely to escape the old belongs there. It is not Earth 2.0, "Now with improved graphics!" It is "new" in a way that will not be held back by our present oldness. And it is old in a way that mocks our modern newness.

It is not heaven we seek *per se*, but the earth-to-come. We were not created for somewhere else. And it's worth noting that God does not seek to merely renovate this earth. John says that the first heaven (sky) and earth "had passed away." It must die and and be resurrected in the pattern of its Creator. What does that say about the change we need to be fit for such a place? We, too, must die and be reborn.

Yes, the Creator isn't done creating yet! This earth-to-come is more than shinier rocks and softer blades of grass. It's new in the kind of way you say your house is new after a much-needed cleaning. You wonder how you ever lived in that old, dirty house for so long without cleaning it. Will we not see this earth-to-come in much the same light? If I could think of one word to describe how I imagine the earth to come to be, it would be "cleaner." But not cleaner in terms of air pollution or trash strewn about. Just... cleaner.

I need clean.

25
Counterfeits

Wolfgang Beltracchi taught me something about counterfeiting. One of the best scam artists and counterfeit painters in the world, he wasn't the best because he made excellent copies of Picasso. He was the best because he could get in Picasso's head and paint something Picasso would have painted. No art collector or museum could look up and say, "Hey, I have the original...this is a fake!" It was an original, after all. The best counterfeits are not cloned copies, but are stamped with the originality of the person's mind.

The dragon knows this, and his counterfeits in Revelation are a mixture of carbon copied miracles and originality meant to make the people think this is God's doing. We see the dragon subtly working behind the scenes, with the two beasts as his agents. Through them, he works miracles, such as bringing fire down from heaven, faking a resurrection, and even giving life to something in his own image. These are all things God has done, and they are difficult to resist believing they are still his doing.

Revelation may be using hyperbole when it says the whole world will worship the beast, but not by much. Use your sacred imagination and put yourself there. Imagine your best friend running up to you with greatest joy — his daughter was miraculously healed of cancer. A man had come in, prayed over her with great agony and sincerity, and she got better! But you've read your Bible, and you know that this wave of religious fervor isn't the "Third Great Awakening," as others have called it. Something seems off about it, and you suspect the devil's hand behind it. But what can you tell your friend? Will you tell him that the miracle was from Satan? If I were him, I'd want to punch you in the face. "My little girl is healed! How dare you say the devil did that! Go read the gospels, dude, and you'll notice that this sort of thing is the work of Jesus. If you claim to follow the Bible, then give me one Bible text that shows this is wrong!" If you're cheeky enough to push the issue, you might push him hard enough to make him say something like, "Fine; the devil healed my girl. Well maybe he deserves my prayers because he's the only one who seems to be doing anything down here."

Look, it's all hypothetical but you get the idea. We are going to have a seriously difficult time pointing out exactly why this miracle is wrong when it has undeniably blessed so many. The time of the end will call for more than smug proof texting. The deceptions seem so intense, and God is so blunt about their success, that it should give us pause. The dragon knows how God works well enough to forge his blessings. We must know the difference between the real and the fake. We must know, as Tolkien says in *Mythopoeia*, that "all that glitters is not gold."

Yet there is so much that is golden in this world, of true worth. Let us be experts in what is real and valuable down here. Treasure what is golden here. Whatever God has touched — that is gold. Gold is best.

The good news is also that every forger messes up at some point. Beltracchi did when he got lazy and bought some store paint instead of making his own. Satan, too, will show his true colors. Knowing that counterfeits are coming puts us on alert.

God will not fail to hold on to you in a time of doubts and deceptions. You will see him walking on the waves even though the storms blow. By faith, you will walk with him.

26
Uncounted

I looked and there before me was the Lamb, standing on Mount Zion, and with him 144,000 who had his name and his Father's name written on their foreheads.

- Revelation 14.1

People make it.

What else needs to be said about the 144,000? Hold the argument about "pre-trib" versus "post-trib" or whether this number is literal or figurative. Those are important questions, but let's first embrace the one point that really has immediate, practical value:

John sees the group of people who make it through the end times.

That is beautiful. We can work ourselves up imagining that the end times are going to the sort of nightmare *1984* would have. We imagine torture and stress and heartache and sometimes all of this can rise like a huge mountain in our imagination so that we cannot see clearly how we get from here to heaven. It's a stormy mess, and all we know is that we have to go through it and that (hopefully) we will somehow find our way when we get there.

But the view of the 144,000 in Rev. 7 and 14 form this magnificent postcard sent back to us from heaven. The picture on the front is of people smiling and singing. And there's not just a few people, either. There are a lot of people who make it through the end. In fact, when John's gaze is drawn from earth to heaven, he sees the same group again, except this time he calls them "a multitude which no one could count" (7.9).

This is the same group, just with before-and-after pictures. The 144,000 represent the group about to be sealed to go through the final conflict. The Great Multitude is the same group after they've gone through the wash, so to speak. They are described to John as having gone through the tribulation, after all, and this is why the 144,000 must be figurative.

Those who make it through the last days comprise a vast horde of faithful ones. They do not stumble out, like our bloodied action hero who came within a hair's breadth of death but managed to prevail. This is not the way of God. With him there are no close victories, only decisive ones. The redeemed do go through as yet unimagined suffering, but they come out singing:

> *They are before the throne of God*
> *and serve him day and night in his temple;*
> *and he who sits on the throne*
> *will shelter them with his presence.*
> *'Never again will they hunger;*
> *never again will they thirst.*
> *The sun will not beat down on them,'*
> *nor any scorching heat.*
> *For the Lamb at the center of the throne*
> *will be their shepherd;*
> *'he will lead them to springs of living water.'*
> *'And God will wipe away every tear from their eyes.'*

> *They sang a new song before the throne and before the four living creatures and the elders. No one could learn the song except the 144,000 who had been redeemed from the earth. These are those who did not defile themselves with women, for they remained virgins. They follow the Lamb wherever he goes. They were purchased from among mankind and offered as first fruits to God and the Lamb. No lie was found in their mouths; they are blameless.*
>
> - Revelation 7.15-17; 14.3-5.

If ever you're tempted to despair, remember: an uncounted throng will march that hard road and emerge on the other side. Let us be glad God did not give us a number, or we should have reason to despair (if we feel it too low) or not adequately prepare ourselves (if we feel most people will be saved). Rather, God told us just enough to give us the hope we need to fuel our faith through such times. Let us be thankful. Let us be there.

Slip that picture in your pocket. Look at it in times of uncertainty or fear. Don't just remember; *imagine* the multitude that no one could count. Hear the song they/we sing. Learn its melody by heart and begin strengthening your voice.

27
Three Angels

Then I saw another angel flying in mid-air, and he had the eternal gospel to proclaim to those who live on the earth.

- Revelation 14.6

God's response to the activities of the beast is to launch three angels, more messengers than missiles. As we've had to come to terms with God's unconventional — that is, undragon-like — methods, we can turn our attention to what the angels have to say.

All three angels are in response to the activities of the beasts and the dragon behind their throne. The first angel is described as having "the everlasting gospel." Forget the loaded meaning behind "gospel" and just take it for its literal value: "Good news." The angel bears good news for the people who have preached the good news to others. We are further told that this angel's good news reaches every corner of the earth. Wherever God's people are, they cannot miss this "loud voice."

The good news is to fear, give, and worship. Those are the three imperatives used in the first angel's super-brief message. Fear God, give him glory, and worship him. This seems a strange, almost fortune cookie-like bit of randomness, until you fit it in its proper context. Down below, the beasts are wreaking havoc. They perform miracles to deceive as many as they can into following the beast. They've threatened God's people with economic hardship and even go so far as to kill them. They want worship. This first angel serves to remind God's people not to fear the beast who threatens them, but to fear the Lord who is greater even than the beasts. As Christians are arraigned in courtrooms, he tells them that God deserves the glory, not these pretenders, because the hour of His judgment — and not the beasts' — has come. As the beasts work their miracles, this angel points to God as uniquely qualified for our worship because he is the Creator. What did the beasts create, after all? Sure, they perform miracles — but didn't Pharaoh's magicians do the same? Show one rock, one tree, one atom they have truly created! They are only agents of destruction and deception like their father, the Dragon. They can only manipulate and corrupt the materials God has created. Don't worship them. They don't deserve it. They're just posers.

To accept the first angel's message requires a lot of faith, however. From our human vantage point, the beasts have absolute control over the world. They kill and embrace whomever they choose. Their reach seems infinite. It'd be really tempting to just cash out and cave in. They have the guns. Where is God, anyway? It will require us to trust like we never have in the invisible and oppressive reality of God. It requires imagination to believe that what cannot be seen is more visible than the pleasant dystopia that Earth becomes.

A second angel follows, telling us that "Babylon is fallen, is fallen." This is a code word to represent the spiritual force of the Dragon in the affairs of men. It is the atmosphere of sin in society. It is the prostitute standing opposed in the valley below God's New Jerusalem. It is the city that has seduced men of power and influence and commerce to live for those qualities alone. Just as she seems to be at her height, invincible in night, the angel emphatically reassures us that what we see isn't all reality. Babylon is as good as fallen. It has happened before by the hand of God's agent, Cyrus (see Isaiah 45:1). God uses the present tense here, saying "has," not "will," to illustrate the certainty of the fall. Though it hasn't happened historically, God is so bent on her destruction that it is as good as done. We mustn't be seduced by her. She hasn't the power she pretends.

The third angel carries the most serious message, which is again aimed at parrying the thrusts of the beasts. This time, we are warned not to accept the mark of the beast. The beast has declared that all who do not receive its mark should die. God's riposte is that all who *do* receive the mark *will* die. While the beast may kill you, God's picture of punishment far exceeds anything the Dragon's henchmen can do. "Do not be afraid of those who kill the body but cannot kill the soul. Rather, be afraid of the One who can destroy both soul and body in hell," Jesus warns us in Matthew 10.28. If you think it's meant to scare you, you'd be correct. It should scare you in the same way that losing a leg is to be feared more than scraping your knee. God is interested in making sure we have our priorities straight. When we do, we can grow. In this upside down world, we are strangely more afraid of the needle than the disease. We must learn to fear the disease more than the needle. Only when we fear God more than the beast can we look the beast in the eye, size him up, and laugh. Why should we fear a house cat when our Lion God stands across the room? Let it scratch!

It is worth remembering that God has the keys to death and Hades. He is not afraid of you dying, and so you and I shouldn't be either. The absolute worst the dragon can do to you is kill you, and in response to that God pronounces a beatitude on those who have died, calling them "blessed." So God turns the Dragon's greatest weapon into a blessing. In this last tempest, death is your "million-dollar wound," as soldiers call it. It is any wound serious enough to send you home but not too serious that you die or are crippled. Death becomes a refuge, a short breather in a long race. This is why the angels' work of keeping us focused on God and not on the beasts is so vital. God has every angle covered, so long as we continue to look to him.

Salvation requires imagination. We must see what cannot be seen and believe what seems impossible to believe. In short, we have to see beyond what we see going around us. There is help past our helplessness. There is justice. There is hope. There is love.

28
Prelude to Plagues

Out of the temple came the seven angels with the seven plagues. They were dressed in clean, shining linen and wore golden sashes around their chests.

- Revelation 15.8

Revelation fifteen is a strange, holy moment of worship — and it's disturbing. We would expect there to be a moment of mournful silence before the plagues fall, not singing and praise. Instead, we see a little praise service, acting like millions of people below aren't about to be painfully tormented. I just want to yell: "I know they deserve it, but show a little class! You don't have to be happy and having a good time about it."

An author means to allow the reader to disappear inside his book, whether fiction or non-fiction. He wants the reader to feel what his character feels, and this emotional bonding between reader and author (via the character) is what makes a book enjoyable. A former president writes his memoirs and wants to place the reader in his shoes to see it from his point of view. But when the author misjudges and doesn't emotionally connect with the reader, it's hard for the reader to go on. It's a huge turn off. You might feel the author is trying to manipulate you if he tries to make you cry over a dead character on the first page. You cannot force these things.

This kind of emotional disconnect is exactly what I think many feel in Revelation 15. The characters are happy, and yet the reader, knowing what will happen to the wicked shortly, doesn't feel the same way. Yes, we're happy Jesus saves his people and the wicked are finally put outside. But we also feel John — or the Holy Spirit — misjudged us, emotionally. He took it for granted that we were on board and that we would join with them in singing and smiling. But that only leaves us grumpy and concerned at having been so poorly understood.

It's partly a misunderstanding on our part. Verse three tells us that the redeemed sing the song of the Lamb and "of God's servant Moses." In the Exodus, plagues fell so that they might free God's people from Pharaoh's grip. God declared at the beginning: "I will lay my hand on Egypt and with mighty acts of judgment I will bring out my divisions, my people" (Ex. 7.3). Each plague gradually turned up the pressure, until Pharaoh finally (and only temporarily) agreed to let God's people go. As a result, the

Lord's people sung a great song of deliverance and praise to the Lord for freeing them from their oppressors.

The rejoicing in Revelation 15 is about celebrating God's impending deliverance of his people from the grip of the beasts and dragon; from all who were then tormenting, hunting, enslaving or trying to deceive his people. He intends these plagues to loosen the grip of the dragon on his people, and this freedom is forever! This is why the angels see this as a holy work. In the vision we see that the heavenly temple is open, including the Ark of the Covenant — and now we can see straight through to the Ten Commandments it contains. These plagues are an act of justice, not revenge. Why should you not rejoice that your God acts in strength to deliver you from the dragon? You see, we cannot have it both ways. In Revelation 13 and 14 we criticize God for acting too weakly in the face of the dragon's onslaught. In Revelation 15 and 16 we criticize him for acting too strongly. And yet we see that every person who would live through those days have nothing but admiration and praise for Christ. The angels who bear the plagues are dressed much as Jesus was in chapter 1, indicating the divine nature of their work.

We fail to connect with the emotions of chapter 15 only when we have not previously identified ourselves with God's people of chapter 13. From our cold, clinical distance high above God, it looks like God is torturing these people. From the ground, as one of his people, it looks like salvation. Praise God! He hasn't forgotten his people!

29
1000 Tears

I saw an angel coming down out of heaven, having the key to the Abyss and holding in his hand a great chain. He seized the dragon, that ancient serpent, who is the devil, or Satan, and bound him for a thousand years.

- Revelation 20.1-2

On paper, the matchup is between some unnamed angel (let's call him "Cadan") of heaven and the great Dragon, the former, fallen guardian to God's throne. In reality, there's no struggle. God's guy glides down here, wraps up the Dragon, and tosses him into the abyss. It reminds me of Guido Reni's gorgeous painting, "Archangel Michael," where Michael serenely holds Satan's chains, steps on his balding head, sword raised to strike the final blow. One angel.

The Dragon's imprisonment is obviously temporary, but necessary (verse 3). God has always meant to rid the universe of sin, not merely quarantine it. The Dragon is incapacitated, paving the way for God to fulfill another promise: letting his people don the gavel and robe of a judge. Those who have been victorious over sin and the beast have been resurrected at Christ's return in order to take their seat:

"I saw thrones on which were seated those who had been given authority to judge"
- Rev. 20.4.

John writes as if we should immediately know who had been given authority to judge. He then specifically names the end-time martyrs as the ones given authority to judge, "reigning with Christ a thousand years." Thus the very people under the fifth seal who prayed for justice are seen here taking the throne to deliver it themselves—and more people besides, if Revelation 5.10 is any guide. Even though Revelation more commonly deals with that final generation that perseveres in the war of the beast, we should expect all who are victorious over sin in any age to sit with Christ on his throne (Rev. 3.21).

In a real sense, the final judgment has been made by Christ. When he returned, he saved some and destroyed others, so obviously he had judged prior to his arrival exactly who had clipped his coupon for heaven. The work of the newly-redeemed at this point is to judge God in a sense. By going back over his judgments, we have the opportunity to quench our doubts. Perhaps we'll find Hitler in heaven and want to know how on earth he made it. Nothing in our human records of him hints at even the slightest regret, let alone repentance. Or maybe we shall think of that pious aunt who isn't present at the call of the heavenly roll. God gives unprecedented access to his record keeper so that we can find closure.

As the problem of Lucifer's rebellion happened in the first place over accusations against God's fairness, God seems to go out of his way to settle all doubts in the end. He offers us total transparency. God wants to give us time to make sure he made all of the right decisions. If you're wondering why he wasn't there at a particular period of your life when he seemed silent, then find out. Every action of God — or seeming inaction — is left for your judgment. This is a judgment of God. We must be assured — not just in faith but in fact — that God did *everything* he could do to save sinners. God is the most public of public figures, and in allowing us to judge him, he allows us to vindicate him. It brings closure to our own stories as well, neatly tying up little doubts and wonderments and enabling the rich life of eternity to begin completely fresh.

30
666

Let the person who has insight calculate the number of the beast, for it is the number of a man. That number is 666.

- Revelation 13.18

Six hundred and sixty six. The mark of the beast. I've been warned that it is a barcode or a tattoo or going to church on the wrong day. Lots of folks using gematria (an ancient system of codes) have added up the letter values of names and fingered people, from Nero to John F. Kennedy as antichrist. Perhaps you already have it? Dozens of websites offer to help you sort it out. I'm sure someone even sells a "mark of the beast removal kit" for six easy payments of $19.99.

The mark of the beast is big business in the book of Revelation, and too many preachers have trafficked in its fear. There are many important issues in Revelation, and the fact that the "number of his name" — 666 — is confined to one verse should tell us a little about its relative importance. What we all can agree upon is that the mark is bad and the true followers of God will shun it. But we must understand a few more basics:

1. The mark isn't given to you against your will. The mark and the seal are symbols of loyalty, given by God and Satan to their followers. God would not let one of his true friends be tricked into joining the devil's side.

2. The mark isn't physical. The mark is only in your hand or forehead, which symbolically represents your actions and your will. You can either be a true believer in the beast and his dragon daddy or you can allow yourself to go with the flow. In contrast, the Seal of God is only seen in the forehead. You must choose to follow God. In Satan's kingdom alone can you be lost by works; in God's realm you must believe.

3. The dragon cannot protect you. Once again, the dragon is counterfeiting God's seal of protection with a mark of his own. The mark is the ultimate members club — without the mark you won't be able to buy and sell. This seems like something we could easily rationalize. We

have to feed our family, after all! God wouldn't want them to starve. But God wins in the end, and Revelation informs us about how dangerous it is to think the devil is as omnipotent as he seems. Following the beast may seem a safer bet — even a noble one — but the fate of the righteous is undiminished life.

4. No one has the mark (or the seal) yet. Stop checking your skin. Dermatologists can't spot it. This is given at the end, in preparation for the last scenes of history. But the distance does not dismiss the urgency. Every choice you make today will chip in, making that final decision for Jesus or Satan that much easier. We deceive ourselves if we are romantically awaiting some critical moment to make a stand for God. Such a moment may never come; or it may come predetermined by a thousand little moments of selfishness. Every choice matters.

5. There are only two options. In the end we must belong somewhere. Like two superpowers pulling smaller countries into their orbit, eventually we must make a decision. There is no neutral. There are no third parties. We see life centralizing around the single most important question left to humans: whom shall we worship? For we certainly must worship.

The number of the name of the beast is part of the puzzle of identifying the beasts, and it isn't even the clearest clue. But if we walk away with a steely determination not to follow the beast, but to claim and be claimed by God, then we have satisfied the Spirit. To think the mark is a barcode or microchip is perhaps exactly the kind of misdirection that best serves the devil, because a person can think they're safe if they avoid it. Safety is only in Jesus, and our focus should be on gazing into his eyes and seeking his approval.

31
Lamb vs Dragon

Then I saw a Lamb, looking as if it had been slain, standing at the center of the throne.

- Revelation 5.6

As we have flown over chapters 12-14 — the heart of the Book of Revelation — we have talked about how chapter 13 is the Dragon's plan of attack while Revelation 14 speaks of God's response. If we're really, really honest with ourselves, we've seem jhpw God's response to the Dragon's attacks seems rather lame.

The Dragon sends two beasts to work miracles and torture and intimidate and persecute and starve and deceive people into worshipping the Dragon.

God's response? To send three angels to yell to the people below.

Don't we often feel that way about God's actions? Wouldn't we rather God grunt a little, deploy his gruff, Austrian accent, and get to work muscling out our problems? Just show a little backbone, God, and be like the superheroes we fantasize about!

Yet the fact that we both understand and even relate better with the tactics of the Dragon should frighten us more. We may grow to disagree with the Dragon's cause, but it's hard to forswear his character. The reality is that we desire the Lamb to be more dragon-like. And this is only because there is part of the dragon within us. He's gotten in, and has changed the way we see things, so that we could be steadfastly on God's side and yet secretly cheer against him. Of course, we don't do this openly and often without realizing it. But we deeply betray the Lord in the way we grumble about his generalship and even wish he were more like the other guy.

But "the other guy" is precisely what we're trying to get away from. I'm afraid that if we want God we have to let God be God. We must learn not to be embarrassed by him. In Revelation 5, we had been led to hope that he would appear as a lion, but we see him as a dying lamb. Weakness. We serve a lamb in the midst of a dragon-war, but that shouldn't worry us because the lamb wins. This calls for us to reevaluate our notions of strength and weakness. Because if we can learn anything about God's strategy in chapter 14 it's that it works.

God sends three angels to deliver in words a counterstroke to the dragon's brute force. What we must conclude from this is that God does not deem the persecution of the dragon through the beasts to be any real danger to us. From his heavenly headquarters, he surveys the battlefield and concludes that all of the enemy's plans are ineffectual. That isn't to say that God's people won't go through some excruciatingly difficult times. But the end result (in verses 14-20) is that the beasts are so easy to topple that Jesus, leisurely sitting on a cloud, just swings his sickle once to save the righteous (leaving a lowly angel to take care of the others with another swipe). Anyone with any pre-Eli Whitney experience with crops — i.e., those in John's day — would laugh at how absurd this is. Two swings?

As I mentioned a few chapters ago, Jesus himself told us to worry not about those who can kill your body, but about him who can throw both body and soul in hell. So all he does is send three angels to reassure God's people that they need to hang on a little longer before he comes. Paul, a man acquainted with great suffering, reassured us all that "the sufferings of this present time are not worthy to be compared with the glory that shall be revealed in us" (Romans 8.37). For Paul, the joy of what is to come will be so amazing that it swallows up everything that's less amazing. Paul — a man beaten, shipwrecked, and bitten by a snake — says, "Guys, heaven will be so great it will make everything we went through forgettable." It's like the kid who whines all of the way to Disney World. "Are we there yet? My phone is dead. My stomach hurts." If that's your kid, then maybe you've seen the magical transformation that takes place when they get in line. "There's Mickey!" Suddenly they're smiling, jumping, taking pictures. . .and you're left wondering when exactly your little stinkbug morphed into a butterfly.

We need to learn to see beyond muscles and threats — even beyond death — and trust that in a battle between a lamb and a dragon, the lamb wins. We need to learn that this upside-down way of living is really right side up.

It's the only way to get to Disney World.

Epi

As the city of Nashville launched its fireworks for their 2014 Fourth of July party, one guy had an idea. He launched his drone high into the night sky, an invisible sentinel over the celebration. The view was incredible. It only got better as he nudged the nose down and parked the drone in the blast area of the fireworks. Streams of sparks shot past the camera with each explosion of color.

It was frightening.
It was beautiful.

The Jesus we see in Revelation is both frightening and beautiful. Jesus is a calamity of hope, the ultimate "eucatastrophe" as Tolkien put it. Jesus is one of the reasons that Revelation is so hard to grasp, because he presents a reality so grotesquely at odds with the *now* we are used to. We can deal with Judases and Caesars, but beasts which kill large swaths of the world population? That seems improbable.

Nevertheless, Jesus is defined in Revelation as the only power capable of rescuing us from such a world. To "water down" the beasts and the idea of global-religious unity against God is to sweep aside the glorious character of Christ. You simply cannot extract the character of Jesus from Revelation without taking all of the other stuff with it, just as surely as you cannot have a Christ without a cross in Matthew.

We're forced then to confront the frightening parts of Revelation in order to enjoy the beautiful. They're handcuffed together. Many of us would prefer a tame beauty of the sort that might fall apart if we are too rough with it. That wish cannot be granted in Revelation, where beauty is richly terrifying. Twice Jesus is depicted as having a sword come out of his mouth. Once he is seen as a bloodied lamb. His eyes are as foreboding as sunlight and he threatens in between promises.

Yet he is worshipped over and over. The more that Jesus intervenes as judge the more the celestial beings heap praise like roses upon the stage after an exquisite performance. This beauty is frightening because it is God's beauty. Now, we are beginning to see God as he is. In this sense Revelation is a masterful unveiling. We've pealed another petal back and we can see further into the presence and beauty of God as we ever could in any other book.

For starters, it puts our prayers into perspective. We were taught to pray for "thy kingdom come" without realizing how dangerous this is. Revelation shows us that the closer Jesus gets to this world, the more the forces of the Dragon are stirred into desperate resistance. To pray for Jesus' kingdom to come to this world is a direct threat to the devil, and he won't let such a thing happen without a fight. We might as well pray for the sun to come closer. For those who aren't completely committed to Jesus, this prayer is suicidal. Revelation forces us to realize that our prayers are ultimately successful. Beyond asking for some help today, we may never grasp the raw power of prayer until we see the sky shredded at the return of its Maker. Prayer is serious power.

Second, we see that Jesus isn't Gandhi. Nor is he "your homeboy," despite what those t-shirts may say. Jesus destroys billions of people in Revelation. *Billions*. Some prefer to see Jesus as a pacifist, taking his "turn the other cheek" teaching as an unwillingness to hurt a fly. Didn't he pray for his persecutors rather than strike back as they nailed him to the cross? Jesus submitted himself to the violence of the cross for the same reason he decimates people in Revelation: to set his people free from sin. In reading Revelation, we cannot fool ourselves as to the real cost of entertaining sin. Yes, God's love for us propelled him to die in our stead at Calvary. But that same love for us also permits him to destroy sinners. You cannot accept the cross without the coming. While we can relate to the human side of Jesus, Revelation reminds us of the Divine wildness that separates him from us. His fire beckons us in from the cold, but it would be foolish to forget that fire still burns those who fail to reverence its nature.

Fire:
Frightening and
Beautiful
      like fireworks.

There are some neighborhoods you just run through.

Revelation is not one of those neighborhoods.

the end

Chrysalis
BALM AND BLADE PUBLISHING

Chrysalis is a branch of Balm and Blade focused on mentoring new and young authors. By guiding writers through the process of preparing a book for publication, our goal is to help them grow and develop their talents, as well as provide an outlet for them to premiere their creative works.

While our primary focus is on new and young authors, Chrysalis is open to anyone looking for a place to grow and develop the wings of their creativity.

Our first Chrysalis author, John Evans, wrote Rising From Perdition during his first three years of high school. Evans draws from his own experiences and dives into the topics of heartache, anger, love, suffering and spirituality. With passion and conviction, he pours his heart out and points us towards the only certainty amidst chaotic flames: Jesus is always with us.

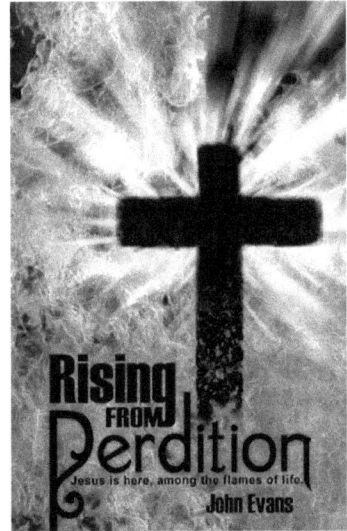

For the latest news and updates
from Balm and Blade Publishing,

please visit us at:
balmandblade.com
facebook.com/balmandblade

BALM AND BLADE
PUBLISHING

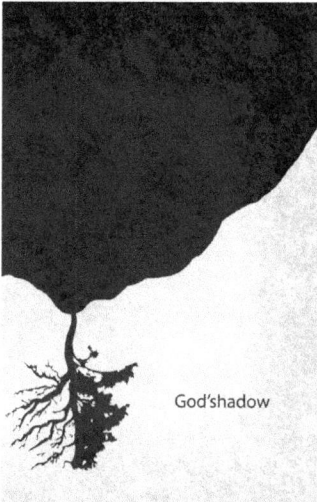

God'shadow || Daniel de Sevén

Daniel de Sevén takes us on journey deeper into doubt through a variety of short, creative essays meant to recall dormant doubts in the reader or else to create new ones. For many it will be an uncomfortable adventure, but it is, the author argues, a necessary one because doubt is the delivery room of faith.

But be warned: this book isn't about the author trying to inductively prove a point. Rather, it is at once disjointed and communal, allowing readers to join the discussion and reach their own conclusions - which the author feels is the only kind of conclusions worth reaching. This isnt teaching; this is discovering.

God'shadow

Shadows and Scars || T. Jason Vanderlaan

"We wander through life, searching for belonging and validation. Here in this valley, we are pursued by the shadows of our regrets and haunted by the scars of our past. We are lost, but in seeking, we will find, and in finding, we will be found."

Shadows & Scars is a messy book. Through poetry, T. Jason Vanderlaan tells a story, but not one that begins in the beginning, or ends at the end. This is about being in the middle, about wandering. This is about loose ends and unresolved issues and the tension of living in the in-between. All the while, dreams of peace and rest float just out of reach – elusive invitations, like fireflies dancing in the summer night.

Within the framework of searching for belonging and validation, Vanderlaan explores a variety of topics – growing up in a divorced family, falling in love, giving and receiving broken hearts, losing the way and finding regret, the ache of letting go, wrestling with forgiveness and hope and trust. When the dust settles, these frayed ends of family, romance, and spirituality tangle together. The result is in an incomplete yet beautiful display, a portrait of the fearful desire to know and be known, to love and be loved, to seek and find and be found.

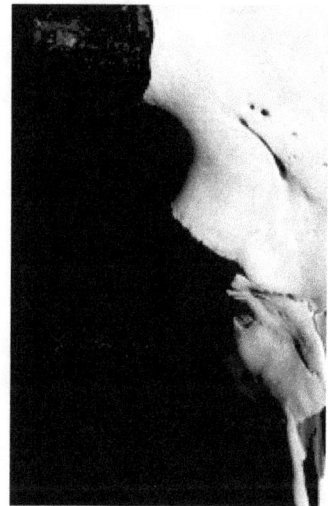

www.ingramcontent.com/pod-product-compliance
Lightning Source LLC
Chambersburg PA
CBHW081250040426
42452CB00015B/2779